THERE IS ONLY AN OPPORTUNITY FOR JUSTICE

BY
JAMES E. CRAWFORD, JR.

JAMES E. CRAWFORD, JR. & ASSOCIATES, LLC
1435 SULPHUR SPRING RD.
ARBUTUS, MD 21227

(443) 709-9999
JUSTICEJEC@COMCAST.NET
CRAWFORDDEFENSEATTORNEY.COM

There Is Only an Opportunity for Justice.
© 2017 by James E. Crawford, Jr.
All Rights Reserved.

ISBN-10: 0-692-83290-4
ISBN-13: 978-0-692-83290-5

The information contained in this book is only general in nature and is not intended to act as specific legal advice. Every legal situation is different, and therefore the information contained herein should not be considered as any form of legal consultation.

Cover photo by Jeff Little.

CONTENTS

Dedication vii
Preface ix
Introduction:
Who Am I, and Why Should You Give a Damn? xiii

Chapter 1:
What Does "Justice" Mean in Our Modern Criminal System? ... 1

Chapter 2:
What Does a Criminal Defense Lawyer Do? 5

Chapter 3:
How Can a Criminal Defense Lawyer Represent People
Who Are Accused of Terrible Crimes? 9

Chapter 4:
Who Gets Charged, and with What Type of Crimes? 13
    Child Porn, Computer, and Sex Crimes   14
    White-Collar Crimes   16
    Theft and Robbery   16
    DWIs and Traffic Violations   17
    Weapons and Violent Crime   19
    Juvenile Crimes   19

Chapter 5:
Overview of the Entire Process 21
    The Investigation Begins   21
    Police and Commissioners   21
    Grand Juries   23
    A "Criminal Information" Charge   23
    Preliminary Hearings   24

Chapter 6:
What Happens after a Summons or Warrant is Issued, and How Does the Bail Process Work? ... 27

Chapter 7:
More about Grand Juries ... 33

Chapter 8:
What Is an Arraignment on the State and Federal Levels? ... 37
    Bail Bonds ... 37
    After the Arraignment ... 40

Chapter 9:
What's the Difference between a Criminal Traffic Charge and a Civil Traffic Citation? ... 43

Chapter 10:
Jury Trials Versus Judge Trials—Which One Do I Choose? ... 45

Chapter 11:
The Defendant's Best Friend: The Fourth Amendment ... 49

Chapter 12:
Sex Crimes ... 55
    Rape in the First Degree ... 57
    Rape in the Second Degree ... 61
    Sexual Offense in the First Degree ... 61
    Sexual Offense in the Second Degree ... 62
    Sexual Offense in the Third Degree ... 62
    Sexual Offense in the Fourth Degree ... 62
    Sodomy ... 63
    Unnatural or Perverted Sexual Practices ... 63
    Sexual Solicitation of a Minor ... 64
    Indecent Exposure ... 65

Chapter 13:
Child Pornography—Remain Calm! ... 69

Chapter 14:
The Sex Offender Registry—Do I Need to Fear It? ... 83

Chapter 15:
How Lawyers and Clients Can Communicate Effectively ... 87

Chapter 16:
If You've Been Charged, Don't Panic! ... 91

Chapter 17:
What Are the Possible Outcomes of My Criminal Case? ... 95
    Not Guilty Verdict ... 95
    Guilty Verdict or Plea ... 96
    Stet ... 97
    Nolle Prosequi (Dismissal) ... 98
    Probation Before Judgement (PBJ) ... 99
    Expungement ... 100

Chapter 18:
Maryland's *Justice Reinvestment Act of 2016* ... 103

About the Author ... 105

Appendix A:
What Crimes Require a Person to Register? ... 113

Appendix B:
Omnibus Motion ... 115

Appendix C:
Maryland Traffic Violation Penalty Quick Reference ... 125

DEDICATION

Dedicated to James E. Crawford, Sr., Esq.
(1941–2009)

My father was a criminal defense lawyer born just as the World War II was beginning. I dedicate this book to him and his memory.

My father taught me many things about life and law. He practiced criminal law from 1961–1998, and he toiled through our court system for his clients like a good lawyer should. I acknowledge the mental and physical toll it took on him throughout the many years when he gave his all to the legal community and his clients. He developed good friends and loyal clients who stuck with him for years. Ever after he died, people I didn't know constantly approached me to tell me courtroom battle stories about him.

Most of his colleagues—including notable lawyers such as Peter Angelos, Thomas Minkin, and Patrick O'Doherty—would agree that Dad had a canny understanding of politics and was one of the most capable people they have ever seen in that arena. From a young age, he participated in Baltimore politics. He ran campaigns and advised prominent political figures. He was a grass-roots, blue-collar politician who knew how to play the game.

In the 1950s, 60s, and into the 90s, the game was "who will endorse whom". Democratic kingpin Harry McGuirk (old "Soft Shoes") ran a political club in Baltimore, and several other politicians did, too. If you planned to run for office and wanted a shot at winning, you needed to get their endorsement. People worked and volunteered for these clubs for years just so they could eventually get an opportunity to run for office. Yes, it was the old Tammany Hall mentality, but it worked for a long time. My father orchestrated many such deals, and people still remember that.

I saw him try cases in the Mitchell Courthouse and kick a little ass along the way. He cared about constitutional principles, and he was a street brawler. He may not have attended Harvard Law School, but he attended the "street" university of hard knocks. I like to think a little of that rubbed off on me.

So, Dad, here is a final "good job" in recognition of the lifetime of devotion you earned. I hope you're practicing law in heaven, or at least arguing for someone who can't defend themselves—just like you did in life.

James E. Crawford, Jr.
2017

PREFACE

Until I was 17, I really believed I would play basketball in the NBA. I played for Mount Saint Joseph High School, which had a very high level of competition, and later at college. Although it may have been unrealistic, I figured if I could think and dream it, then I could make it happen! It was my life, and I lived and breathed it every day. As a kid, I spent up to ten hours a day playing outside on the courts with the older, bigger guys, trying to show them up—which, quite honestly, I did many times. Even though others would tell you I was pretty damn good for a skinny 6'3" or 6'4" kid (depending on if I was wearing my "Chuck Taylor" Converse shoes) from Irvington in Baltimore City, I realized the dream wasn't going to happen. Some things in life just aren't meant to be.

But along with that burning desire for sports, I wanted to do something big, something really astounding. That became law school. Since I couldn't become Pete Maravich on the basketball court, I decided to become that same guy in our judicial courts and represent people who needed my help. I needed to find a way to transform my ball-handling skills into speaking skills. I figured, "What the hell? How hard can it be?"

I learned just how hard it could be. Practicing law can be one of the toughest and most grueling professions in our society. To be the best in any profession takes skill, determination, willpower, and guts. I learned from the ground up, from notable lawyers such as Peter Angelos, Patrick O'Doherty, and, of course, my father. I learned from my law professor Byron Warnken, who is truly one the most outstanding lawyers and people of his generation. I learned tricks of the trade from countless judges over the years—and from my clients, too! Long ago, I received sage advice from a well-known politician you would recognize if I told you his name. He said, "Jim, it's the person who constantly reinvents himself that ultimately becomes successful." I took that to heart and reinvented myself as a lawyer.

My skills as a lawyer include the ability to explain and impart knowledge to others. In this book, I explain the basics of law. I've sorted them into chapters so that someone involved with the criminal justice system can go right to the information they need. If you are in a stressful legal situation, the principles and information in this book will help you, and they will shed light on our criminal justice system; specifically, the State of Maryland and the Baltimore federal District Court system.

By having a basic understanding of the judicial process, you will gain clarity about how to navigate your situation. The more you understand the process, the more it can be steered to a successful conclusion. By understanding the mechanics and thought processes behind the system, both clients and lawyers will be better equipped to have productive discussions with about solving their dilemmas.

I have practiced law in Maryland for 26 years, and toiling in our various state courts has taught me many things. I believe wholeheartedly in the enduring tradition that lawyers absolutely protect their clients at all cost. I also believe it is a privilege and honor to represent clients in our American judicial system, and that lawyers owe a certain duty not only to their clients but to the system itself. Without this system, there is no opportunity for justice.

The American judicial system is the greatest system ever invented. It regulates and administers a justice and fairness in our society. But, it is merely a tool and, like any tool, can be used for purposes other than what it was made to do. While our judicial system can be a means of advancement and betterment, it is undoubtedly flawed. It is an adversarial system where the best, smartest, and strongest party wins the day.

What does "win the day" mean? It could mean the defendant you are representing is found not guilty. It could mean that the state's attorney or the United States Department of Justice decides to dismiss a case or a count in an indictment. Or, it could simply mean that your client received a great deal in sentencing or in some other finalization of the case. "Winning" can mean many things, and what it means to the defendant is determined individually, by each person.

Hence, the reason I choose to call this book *There Is ONLY an Opportunity for Justice* is that each individual case and each individual situation is truly an island unto itself. Large-scale prejudicial factors may influence a case's outcome. As I tell my clients, there is no guarantee of justice in any situation. There is only a *chance*, thereby creating an *opportunity* for justice. And if we dig deeper, what does "justice" mean anyway? Do we want a dispensation of justice that is fair? I think so. But in many of our minds, an outcome is only fair if we "win".

After considering the facts in this book, you must make your own decision about what justice really means. My conclusion, after many years of practice, is that justice can only be defined individually by each participant in each case. Justice, after all, is the orphan of many philosophers over the centuries, and I am modest enough to realize I can't cover all its meaning here.

This book should not to be construed as legal advice, because every situation is different. This book merely illustrates the process that a typical criminal defendant will experience. However, it is also an easy guide and navigation tool for people who are looking for a specific subject to research and understand.

I want to acknowledge all the lawyers, prosecutors, public defenders, judges, and professors who have influenced me not only by setting examples but by laboring every day in our Maryland courts for the citizens of this great state. Few people realize what lawyers go through emotionally and physically. Law practice takes a toll on the body and mind, and we all pay a price in some way. But, the legal community known as the Maryland bar always rises to the challenge.

Finally, to my past clients and future clients, I truly hope this information helps your cause, just as I have always worked to help you as your criminal defense lawyer.

INTRODUCTION:
Who Am I, and
Why Should You Give a Damn?

I'm a lawyer—but who cares, right? There are a million lawyers out there, and a million more who don't seem to give a damn about what they do. I've seen it, you've seen it, and the whole world has seen it. What's different about me, if anything?

If you asked that to my face, I would say, "Nothing." But my clients would you tell you that I'm one of the lawyers who *does* give a damn. I've been a scrapper, working the system to get great results for my clients. I'm proud of that.

Believe it or not, many lawyers work for years below the radar and put in countless hours to help their clients. They include both prosecutors and defense lawyers. Both play a pivotal part in the societal game called "trying to get a just result". I've often been asked why I became part of this profession and what drives me to help people in their time of need. After all, it can sometimes be a thankless job. But other times, it's the greatest job on Earth!

I'll tell you a story of being a little boy in Baltimore in the 1960s. I used to hold my father's hand and travel with him to all the courts and sit in on countless client consultations. I watched so many jury and court trials that I became known around the courthouses. As a boy, I didn't understand the full context of what was being said, but I did understand some basics. The more I observed these consultations and how my father interviewed potential criminal and civil clients, the more I realized how much those people really needed him.

My father, James E. Crawford, Sr., grew up in Baltimore and became a prominent political figure as a young man. He practiced law with some of the best judges and prosecutors in Baltimore's history in the 1960s, 70s, and 80s. I learned a lot from him. One of the things I learned was that sometimes a forceful attitude is necessary, but other times a graceful, eloquent attitude does the trick. A lawyer's bedside manner can be just as important as a doctor's.

My greatest memory of a consultation was when a mother and father in their sixties came into Dad's office to talk to him about their son. They were nice people, Greek immigrants who spoke broken English. They had come to the USA years before. And though they still held on to many of their traditional, cultural values, I could tell they were proud to be American. They had raised their one and only son as best they could.

As I listened, I realized they had worked their fingers to the bone running a restaurant they had established years before. A small breakfast diner, it was well-known in west Baltimore and employed a handful of locals. But the husband and wife did most of the work, often for 18 hours a day. They lived at the diner and worked their asses off to provide for their son.

They tried to get him into a great college, but he wasn't following their lead. They may have spoiled him because they wanted so badly for him to succeed and have what they didn't have. They over-provided for him, but he didn't really appreciate what they were doing. Even at my young age, I knew from what I was hearing that he was a spoiled brat.

The wife had callused knees. They almost looked deformed from her working on them all those years scrubbing the floors in the restaurant's kitchen. She got out of her chair and walked around the desk to Dad. She sobbed hysterically and begged Dad to help her. She got down on her callused knees and put her hands together, as if in prayer. She said, "Please do everything you can to help my only son... *Please.*"

It was like a bolt of lightning struck me. I felt a surge of energy and adrenaline like the kind that allows a parent to lift a car off a child. I realized that at that moment, no one else on Earth could help their son more than my father.

The husband grabbed his wife and held her. Dad talked with them for a long time about what to do. They left with a game plan and total confidence in my father. He had a great bedside manner!

The case went on for months, and I attended the trial. Dad spoke to the jury in a soft monotone at first, and eventually ended in a fit of rage, bellowing out that the allegations made against this young man were false. His loud voice carried so clearly that people came in from the hallway to listen. He demonstrated that he believed in his client and that a wrong had been perpetrated here.

I watched him prepare for the case, obtain the services of experts, and cross-examine police officers. He was amazingly effective at questioning each witness to get to the heart of the matter. After a two-day trial, Dad and his young defendant sat at the trial table as the jury walked into the courtroom, which became deathly silent. I looked at each juror, trying to anticipate what they would say in the next minute. But I got no clue! Only later in my career did I develop ways to detect jurors' body language.

Other lawyers had told me that if each juror looks at the defendant as they walk into the courtroom, the defendant will most likely be exonerated. If the jurors do not look at the defendant, then they feel guilty about the verdict. On that day, not one juror looked at my father's client. My heart sank as they sat in the jury box. I can still hear the judge, a prominent man I was lucky enough to get to know very well later in life, say, "Ladies and gentlemen of the jury, have you reached a decision?"

The foreman stood. As if in slow motion, he turned to look directly into the defendant's eyes. "We find the defendant not guilty." The young man's parents looked as if a dagger had been removed from their hearts, and they took a deep breath. Now they could live.

The young man held out his hand to my father, who shook it. Dad made it seem as if it was no big deal, just another day on the job. But I knew he was proud of what he did. When he walked out of the courtroom, the rest of the family tearfully thanked him for his work.

There was no press. There was no story written about the case, and no video or television appearance. There was only the defendant, his lawyer, the state's attorney, the jury, and a judge.

It was then that something changed in me. I realized that the power to divert a government prosecution and help an innocent person is a greater power than any amount of money or a prestigious job.

That young man went on to accomplish many great deeds in life. He realized the gift he had been given—not just through his parents, but a life-changing event that was directed, produced, and effectuated by his lawyer!

Think about it. A state's attorney tried to prosecute this young man with all the awesome might and power of the state government behind him. The state had all the resources and all the people to assist the prosecuting attorney in convincing 12 people that this defendant was guilty. Dad, as one criminal defense attorney, had only the power of two immigrant parents behind him. But with mind, his guts, and his ability to speak directly to the jury, he thwarted the state's wrongful prosecution of this young man.

At that moment, I knew I would be a criminal defense attorney for the rest of my life.

Dad died eight years ago. And though he had been unable to practice law for several years because of health reasons, he taught me a lot about his technique. In some ways, we differ in our practice of law. Although I incorporated his love, drive, and stamina during criminal jury trials, I also use more modern methods to succeed. But his work ethic and thought processes in that young man's case propelled me to law school and helped me become the lawyer I am today.

I humbly try to carry on that experience and teach the lawyers in my firm those same feelings and thought processes about representing a defendant. Since that case, I've met many more people who feel anxious about trying to rescue their child or loved one from going to jail. It is often a matter of life and death. Until you have lived through a situation where the government is trying to take away your liberty, you cannot truly realize what a grim prospect it is.

If you aspire to practice criminal law and defend people, be advised that it takes more than years of school and knowledge. It's about protecting constitutional principles and, while doing so, helping people in their daily lives.

I don't doubt that many people I represent are guilty. It's not my job to cast judgement on what they did or didn't do. The principle is simple: Who can and will stand between the government and a person who is charged with a crime? Who makes the prosecution jump through *all* the hoops before it can get a conviction? Who stands beside a person in their darkest moments to give them the utmost attention and skill when they are facing the gallows?

It is, of course, the American trial lawyer. We are a special breed. But that's what we were born to do!

1
What Does "Justice" Mean in Our Modern Criminal System?

Why are Americans so infatuated with justice? Are we so invested in the idea that somebody is always trying to screw us over that we are constantly blaming others? Do any of us really know what justice stands for?

Every day, on the news and social media, we hear cries of "injustices" being perpetrated upon us by a multitude of culprits. In criminal matters, the dialogue is inevitably pushed toward how police don't treat us justly. The pontification on racism and discrimination inevitably turns to governmental and societal wrongs. It seems we believe everyone, all the time, is trying to get over on us somehow.

Guess what? We may be right! We are a society of people for whom the constant dose of injustice does not go down well. That's good. It means that despite the fact that many only see justice from their perspective, society's dispensation of justice will slowly work its way to equality and perfection.

The word "justice" is derived from old French, which was in turn derived from the Latin words *iustitia* and *iustus*. Though the meaning has evolved over the centuries, the word has always referred to equity, vindication, courts of justice, and judging equally.

When I think of justice as a criminal defense lawyer, I think of a court of law where the results are fair, moral, and equitable. I expect our courts to hand out moral and fair judgements in our criminal cases.

But as we all know, defendants do not always receive "fair and just" criminal sentences. Why does it seem like some people get better deals than others? Many people point the finger at lawyers and defendants who have enough money to spend on experts, forensics, investigations, and jury preparation to slow down the prosecution and get a desired result. Much of that is true.

Having practiced law as a criminal defense attorney for 26 years, I believe there is no "right" to justice in our society. Experience has taught me that we only have the right to try and obtain justice by any means necessary within our court system.

I've seen it all, from speeding ticket cases to notorious murder cases, from sex offenses and child porn to domestic assaults—just to name a few. I've handled all of them for years. And in all that time, I've struggled to figure out what "justice" means. It's taken me many years to come to the conclusions I have. It has taken years of jury trials, looking at witnesses on the stand who I know are lying through their teeth, and trying to find the truth for my client. Yes, it has been often frustrating, but rewarding overall!

Justice clearly means different things to different people. Recently, in Baltimore we had a situation where the defendant Freddy Gray was arrested on misdemeanor charges. While he was being transported to the Baltimore Jail Booking Center, he died. There was an immediate uproar in the Baltimore community, and riots ensued for several days. Baltimore's state's attorney quickly indicted six police officers on various charges.

Mr. Gray represented different things to different people, but he was undoubtedly a controversial figure. His rap sheet was twice as long as his arm. He was a well-known local who was locked up many times for petty and sometimes serious drug charges. The Baltimore community cried out for "justice" for Freddie after his arrest and death march to the Baltimore city jail. He was apparently injured before he was put into the police paddy wagon and transported. Somehow, tragically, he died during transport.

After the first police officer who was charged ended up having his case dismissed, the remaining five also received the same fate. Many people in Baltimore and throughout the country felt it was an unjust decision. But the police officers and many people in the law-enforcement community felt it was, in fact, a just decision.

The point is that justice is a matter of perception, in many ways like your preference for an ice cream flavor. Undoubtedly, there are universal ideas that bind basic rights and beliefs to justice; but in many cases, justice is an opinion. You may have a deep belief in what justice means in a situation, but guess what? My belief may be different. Justice may simply mean that your team won!

Most people who come to my office and are charged with a crime are simply interested in having their situation taken care of in a way that best suits them. Quite often, they are already locked up, and their family comes to my office. If they have several previous criminal charges, they are typically only interested in getting out and staying out of jail. Other people are extremely worried about having any kind of criminal charge on their record.

The point is that justice may mean many different things to many people. But to the people who have a major hurdle in front of them such as a criminal charge, justice can be defined as taking care of the problem at hand!

The reality is that most people are simply scared to death when they are charged in a criminal case. They have no idea what to do or how to act when they are charged by a person or a police officer. Justice is a very narrow act to them. They scream, "Just get me out of this, Mr. Crawford!"

I get it. I do. And I dutifully start down that path!

2
What Does a Criminal Defense Lawyer Do?

A criminal defense lawyer must wear many different hats, but I view my job as straightforward and simple. I stop the government from successfully prosecuting you! Countless media and regular people have asked me exactly what I do and how I do it. My answer? I give people back their lives!

TV shows and books have stereotyped defense lawyers. While some of the stereotypes are realistic, many are not. The lawyer's role has evolved over the years and, depending on what court is involved, the role may shift.

The first thing I do when a client comes to my office is greet them and get to know them personally. I assess their situation and get into the facts of the case. I pick apart every detail. All good criminal defense lawyers will then analyze the law and carefully apply it to the facts presented.

The heart of the matter is what I'm after. I'm not necessarily worried about the defendant's actions, although they are relevant. What I really want to see is if the government can prove each and every element of their case against my defendant. Because if they can't, then the case will go away.

During this initial discussion, I might not ask for the defendant's version of the story. Why? The reason has to do with ethics and the fact that a criminal lawyer can unwittingly and severely handicap a defendant early on if she is not careful.

For example, if a client tells me they committed a crime, it is unethical for me to allow the client to testify at the trial that they did not. The American Bar Association and the Maryland State Bar Association specifically require candor and truthfulness from lawyers. Hence, a lawyer cannot knowingly allow a client to testify untruthfully.

However, a skillful defense attorney will say to a criminal client that his or her version of the events is not always applicable or immediately relevant. In other words, I don't ask for a denial from the client. Sometimes I do ask for the whole story, but many times it is not necessary right away.

I have handled thousands of cases ranging from simple traffic misdemeanors to major felonies, so I know how to "direct traffic" in an interview with a client. I can quickly figure out whether the state or federal government has a case against my client.

The primary job of a criminal defense lawyer is to advise a client. Advice can mean explaining the law, what the chance of success are, what could happen in their situation, and the judicial process.

Lawyers play a special role in society when they help people who find themselves accused of a crime. A criminal defense lawyer stands in the defendant's place in a court of law. There aren't many forums in this world where a person can completely represent another person for what they did or didn't do. A fantastic local lawyer who had practiced law for 40 years once taught me that despite the way society may feel about lawyers, we serve a purpose that is instrumental to the function of the judicial system. Our clients undoubtedly need us.

That lawyer told me a story about a person who was charged with a crime and was later deemed innocent. During the original case, this person had no one to stand beside them. In fact, everyone hated him for the sex crime he allegedly committed. In our society, as soon as someone is alleged to have committed such an act, almost everyone turns against them. Even the defendant's family turned against him, and he had no one to turn to but his lawyer.

You may say that the lawyer is paid money to perform a service, and that is true. But money can be overrated when you're dealing with high-stress, high-stakes cases. A good defense attorney will stand side-by-side with the defendant and fight with every iota of their soul. Sometimes, all the defendant has is his lawyer.

The point my friend was making is this: The biggest role criminal defense lawyers play is advocating for someone who has been *accused* of a crime, but not convicted! There's no question that my job as a lawyer is to push back against the state's attorney prosecuting the case as well as the Department of Justice—and the court, too. A lawyer should set the tone of the proceedings and steer them in a successful, winning direction.

I'm often told that after practicing for the amount of time I have that every piece of me is a lawyer. And it's true. I live, breathe, and sleep law. It becomes part of you, and part of your very soul. I see it in many good lawyers. The process of defending becomes part of them, and everything they do in their life is justice personified.

Lawyers can also be defined by the courts where they practice. Different courts mean different procedures, and some are more complicated than others. Our criminal court system in Maryland is basically broken into four different courts: The District Court, Circuit Court, Court of Special Appeals, and the Court of Appeals.

The District Court is "the people's court". (At least that's what the Baltimore City Courthouse on Fayette Street is called.) It's the court where traffic cases, misdemeanors, and a limited scope of felonies are heard. No jury trials occur there. As soon as a jury trial is requested (if the defendant is subject to 90 days incarceration or more), then the District Court loses jurisdiction to the trial court, called the Circuit Court.

Some cases tried in the state's District Courts can be relatively simple. A lawyer might not need to do much research; she only needs to gather the facts and potential witnesses. Sometimes, a lawyer can literally "walk into" the courtroom and take care of it. But, this is usually not the case. A good criminal defense lawyer is always prepared by knowing the law, the facts of the case, who the prosecutor is, and what the likely outcome is in front of a specific judge.

The Circuit Court has been called the "court where the real action is". All the serious cases are tried there, sometimes in front of a jury and sometimes only a judge. Some misdemeanor and appealable traffic cases are also heard there. It takes a defense lawyer with a considerable amount of knowledge and skill to master this court.

All these considerations are discussed with the client. A client should be well aware of what the possible outcomes are. He should be advised of the specifics of each court. Lawyers must make it clear that although we cannot guarantee the result, we will fight for a successful result for the client. Every time I step into a courtroom, I feel I am protecting the Constitution of the United States and the Maryland Declaration of Rights.

3

How Can a Criminal Defense Lawyer Represent People Who Are Accused of Terrible Crimes?

As Johnny Cash sang, "I've been everywhere, man." I have represented people in all kinds of cases over the years—from speeding tickets all the way to murder. And I am constantly asked how the hell I can represent people who are accused of some of the crimes people see on the news. Many of the crimes are very serious, even heinous. Most people who ask me that question come from the media or government, and almost all are people who have never been charged with a crime themselves!

Hollywood has perpetrated the myth that defendants who are accused of a crime are not guilty. It makes for a good detective story, but isn't reality. However, there is a dichotomy. I often suggest my clients to go to Baltimore city jail, open the gate, and yell, "Hey! How many of you guys and gals are innocent?" My clients laugh because they think the answer is obvious: The people in jail are guilty. But I tell my clients they are very wrong about that. The percentage of people sitting in jail who did not commit the crime of which they are accused is astounding! The reality is that some are guilty and some are not, and that's why we have prosecutors and defense lawyers to battle it out.

It's not my job as a criminal defense lawyer to judge people about what they have or have not done. Many times, defendants feel justified in what they've done, and many people swear to me that they are innocent. I don't always believe them, but often I do. The point is that your moral calibration is not important to me from a criminal-defense standpoint. In other words, whether you did the crime or not isn't the important thing here. That's between you and an entirely different person: your priest, rabbi, or minister!

The job of the state and federal governments is to charge people with crimes and, if they are convicted, to keep them away from the rest of society. That usually means jail. My job as a criminal defense lawyer is to make sure the government must jump through every hoop and climb every possible mountain to get a conviction in your case.

In developing the principles of the Declaration of Independence, the Constitution of the United States, and the Maryland Declaration of Rights, the founding fathers knew the secret! The secret is not about morality. It's about corruption in government. My job is to protect and defend the principles established by our rule of law. "Let no person be unjustly accused and convicted" is the cry for liberty and justice. It's an awesome responsibility and may be one of the most important tasks in keeping our republic true. It isn't about a particular person or a particular case. A lawyer's job is to simply protect the public and the people from being prosecuted indiscriminately.

If criminal defense lawyers in our society do not hold a prosecutor's feet to the fire, what's to prevent them from prosecuting anyone they want for any arbitrary purpose? History is filled with governmental abuses of power such as creating false crimes against innocent people or groups. If someone in the government doesn't like you, then guess what? If there is no rule of law, then the government can prosecute you at its whim for whatever reason it wants.

Criminal defense lawyers in our society protect the citizenry from arbitrary prosecution. That's why it is so important that our judges be completely independent from government and not be able to participate in our political process except when they are specifically elected. The way I see it, my job is to fight the government *on each and every case*, even if the client is guilty. Because if the government can't jump through the hoops and prove their case, then it is better to let ten guilty people go free rather than convict one innocent person. As John Adams believed, requiring the government to prove every bit of the case beyond a reasonable doubt and with moral certainty is of the utmost importance!

I want to tell you a story about a series of cases in a Maryland jurisdiction to illustrate how frivolous and inequitable cases are sometimes resolved. I won't mention the jurisdiction because it would unfair to the judges and state's attorneys as well as the public defenders.

My office represents many defendants who have been charged with sex offenses, including possession, distribution, and manufacturing of child pornography. A county in Maryland had established a policy that all people charged with possession or distribution of child pornography would receive an offer for a plea deal prior to any forensics information being tested by state laboratories. That's important because the evidence isn't always what it appears to be. The plea offers usually included at least 18 months in the local detention center as well as major probation and Tier 1 registration in the sex offender registry. Those offers have extremely serious ramifications for the defendants and will affect them for the rest of their lives.

My job as a criminal defense lawyer was to find a way to pierce that veil. The state's attorney would argue to most defense lawyers that if the plea was not taken, then the file would be sent to the federal District Court, assuming the Department of Justice would take the case; and if so, then any conviction would include a mandatory five years in prison (which it does not in state court). Hence, the state's attorney's office attempted to "handcuff" the defendant into taking a plea to get rid of the case.

Even though child pornography is a terrible crime and has major ramifications on children and society, it is a criminal defense lawyer's job to make sure that he or she does everything possible to prevent any conviction. Instead of taking the easy way out and accepting the plea, I decided in all these cases to simply go to trial.

As I expected, the state's attorney's office sometimes had a very difficult time getting a conviction in these cases and winning before a jury. Many things come into play, such as computer forensics and experts. As a result, I got great outcomes for my clients. Many prosecutors throughout the state now know I will try these cases, and so they are not so quick to make an unreasonable offer.

Many state's attorneys were upset that we held their feet to the fire, and many felt justified in being harsh in these situations because of the nature of the crime. But as I've explained, my job is not to pass judgement on the crime but to prevent the government from getting a conviction.

I've taken that same fundamental thought process and applied it to all my firm's criminal defense strategies throughout the state of Maryland and in federal District Court. Because our system is an adversarial system where one party succeeds and the other one doesn't, it's extremely important to use every resource available!

4
Who Gets Charged, and with What Type of Crimes?

Who gets charged with crimes? More than half of society! My primary office is right outside Baltimore, and I have satellite offices throughout the state of Maryland, so I see many people who get charged with crimes. To simplify things, I have listed nine *basic* criminal activities in Maryland. There is no shortage of defendants being accused of these crimes!

1. **Sex crimes:** Including rape, sexual assault, child pornography, prostitution, indecent exposure, statutory rape, solicitation, sex abuse, sodomy, and third- and fourth-degree sex offenses, and sex offender registration.
2. **Computer crimes:** Including possession and distribution of child pornography, chat room offenses, computer tampering, identity theft, piracy and file-sharing, and copyright infringement.
3. **White-collar crimes:** Including mortgage and other types of fraud, tax evasion, and theft by deception.
4. **Theft and robbery:** Including shoplifting, larceny, robbery, and burglary.
5. **DWI/DUI and traffic violations:** Including drunk driving, driver's license suspension, and traffic violations.
6. **Drug charges:** Including drug possession, possession of drug paraphernalia, drug distribution, and drug kingpin charges.
7. **Weapons and violent crimes:** Including assault and battery, weapons charges, carjacking, arson, manslaughter, and homicide.
8. **Family and domestic cases:** Including domestic violence, *ex parte*/protective orders, child abuse, and child endangerment.

9. **Juvenile cases:** Including underage drinking and other charges faced by people under the age of 18.

Child Porn, Computer, and Sex Crimes

Sex crimes are always a hot topic for discussion. They include rape, sexual assault, child pornography, prostitution, indecent exposure, statutory rape, solicitation, sex abuse, sodomy, third- and fourth-degree sex offenses, and sex offender registration.

Although these crimes do not fit any one pattern, I have for many years represented older males with no prior criminal history regarding child pornography. Child pornography is a unique type of criminal offense and has been labelled and categorized throughout this country. Years ago, Congress enacted federal legislation that defined child pornography. In essence, child pornography is the capturing, possessing, and creating of any images or video of a person under 18 years of age.

The Maryland statutes specifically indicate that if you are on your computer and you run across such images, you must delete them immediately. If you do, then no crime has been committed. I've interviewed many people who view child pornography, and I have found that many have diagnosed or undiagnosed depression and other psychological or mental disorders. However, these crimes are often committed on a whimsical basis without any intent to break the law. Federal and state statutes specifically indicate that possession and/or manufacturing of the images is a crime.

There is a major distinction between simple possession and distribution. If you are downloading images or video of child pornography, and your software has the capacity to "share" images or video, most jurisdictions—including Maryland—will label that as "distribution".

At the federal level, a conviction of a distribution charge results in a mandatory five years in federal prison. On a state level, the sentence can often be reduced to simple possession and/or no jail time. It depends on the situation, the jurisdiction, and ultimate outcome of the case. Convictions for other sex crimes such as rape and sexual assault carry a requirement for sex offender registration.

Allegations of sex crimes often follow situations where alcohol was involved. Many times, a male may believe that a female is consenting to the crime; but afterwards, when the female realizes what happened, she determines that she did not consent. In these situations, judgement is a balancing act. As I explain to all young people, you take a major risk if alcohol or drugs are involved in a situation like this! Literally. your life and freedom could be at stake.

In all sex offense cases, one of the most powerful deterrents and painful punishments is registration in the state's sex offender database. Many people are more worried about being in the registry than being in prison. The Maryland sex offender registry consists of three tiers. Tier 1 is a 15-year mandatory requirement to register. Tier 2 is a mandatory 25-year commitment to register, and Tier 3 is a lifetime commitment.

Many actions can be taken, such as trying to obtain a probation before judgement or winning the case to prevent the defendant from needing to register. Probation before judgement means the judge strikes the guilty verdict and there is no conviction. I have been very successful in helping my defendants to adequately prepare for their case by taking certain pretrial classes and completing psychological and sexual evaluations before stepping into a court room.

It is important to give the judge a known quantity about the defendant, such as whether that person is classified by an expert as being likely or unlikely to commit a similar sexual act in the future, or is even classifiable as a pedophile. Does the defendant have the propensity to commit this type of crime again? This information drastically influences the judge and the state's attorney as to their recommendation in the case, and the ultimate sentencing.

White-Collar Crimes

White-collar crimes are one of the fastest growing areas of criminal activity in this country. These cases are usually charged in federal court but are becoming more and more common in state courts. They include mortgage fraud, tax evasion, employment fraud, and social security fraud. On the federal level, some of these crimes carry major penalties which are much harsher than on the state level. On the state level, these things can often be worked out with a payment plan for restitution, because the individual usually commits the crime due to economic problems.

Theft and Robbery

Theft and robbery cases have been around for a long time: shoplifting, larceny, good old-fashioned theft, stealing from one's employer, robbery, and burglary.

Judges throughout the state *really* dislike burglary cases. Put yourself in the shoes of a judge. If someone has the audacity to break into a house, whether the owners are home or not, and encroach on their privacy, then that burglar is a dangerous person! The threat hits hard because no one wants it to happen to them. Judges have feelings, too! It's about the principle of the sanctity of one's own home.

Many judges give harsh sentences on these cases, so it's important to expose the judge to the problems in the defendant's life: drug use, personal problems, and financial issues. Many of these cases are won long before the case even starts, because the lawyer has done her homework! Many are very difficult to prove by the state unless there is forensic evidence such as fingerprints, DNA, or eye witnesses. Pawn shops play a role in exposing defendants, because that's how many of them get money for their stolen goods.

Shoplifting is one of the most interesting types of theft I have dealt with. I have handled thousands of shoplifting cases. Most of them are "suicide by shoplifting", because many shoplifters aren't doing it for profit. They don't really want or need the stuff. At least

70% of the people I see charged with this crime have money in their pocket and can pay for the items they allegedly stole. They are in very stressful situations in their lives, and shoplifting is a call for help, whether they realize it or not.

Many stay-at-home moms go through this, as well as high-powered executives. Even high-profile athletes and politicians do it. It's often about the thrill of getting away with the crime. It serves as a temporary release from what's going on their lives. It is rarely thought out or analyzed by the shoplifter, but it becomes a habit or a dare in their minds, or even an addiction.

I also see people who are "boosting" simply to get money to buy drugs or other items on a daily basis. This often happens in stores like Home Depot, Office Depot, and other places where merchandise is easily returned and exchanged. Many drug addicts are caught shoplifting quite a few times, and it becomes their way of life until the addiction and their underlying psychological problems are taken care of.

DWIs and Traffic Violations

The most infamous type of traffic violation is the DWI. DWIs in Maryland have hit an all-time high in recent years. Many are even committed on federal properties such as Fort Meade and other federal highways. If you are caught on a federal highway with alcohol in your system—or any other type of illegal substance—you will be charged in a federal court.

A first-time DWI can be resolved and modified to a point where it will not seriously affect a person most of the time, but much work must be done to make this happen smoothly. A typical DWI is very easy for a state or federal government to prove. However, the most common way I attack a DWI charge is to question the stop itself and raise Fourth Amendment concerns about probable cause.

I've handled thousands of DWIs in my career, and I can tell people what the statement of charges says almost verbatim before I even read it. The state and county police are taught how and what to say to effectively prosecute a DWI case. The case usually begins with police stopping a vehicle for speeding, weaving, or some other traffic offense. Nine times out of ten, officers will report that upon approaching the vehicle they immediately smelled alcohol on the driver's breath or in the vehicle. Officers usually report it as a moderate or heavy odor.

The officer may then detain the driver and investigate whether the person is driving under the influence of alcohol or another substance. The roadside investigation usually includes the field sobriety test: the one leg stand, the walk and turn, the horizontal gaze nystagmus, and the alphabet test. The detainee is then taken to the station to test blood alcohol content (BAC). The detainee is read their DR15 rights (right to refuse the BAC test) and sometimes Miranda rights depending on what they are being charged with. Remember this: Anyone charged with DWI with a Maryland license, including a CDL, only has ten days to request a hearing with the Office of Administrative Hearings if they want to continue driving after the forty-fifth day after the stop. It's the details that count!

DWI charges are attacked successfully in a couple different ways. First, the defendant must be very diligent in getting involved in a certified drug and alcohol class to show the court there are no other issues in their life, and that this occurrence was just a glitch. I also have defendants read a book that has been around for 25 years called *Above the Influence*, which many judges use in "baby judge school". It makes the defendant appear to be diligently attempting to correct and educate themselves about the situation. The book is actually very informative.

The whole goal in a DWI is to keep the points off your record and avoid a criminal conviction. In the back of this book, I've included a two-page worksheet I developed as a checklist of things for defendants to do before and after trial. These are tools and resources that help prepare my clients for court. I call it my "prescription page" because it prescribes remedies for the DWI situation.

Weapons and Violent Crime

Charges about weapons and violent crimes are on the rise in Maryland. The state has become very tough on gun possession and weapon charges, and I see many DWI charges tied to weapons charges. For example, an driver arrested for a DWI may have a weapon in their vehicle, which is subsequently discovered by a police officer when the vehicle is searched.

If the weapon was used in a violent crime, then there are very serious potential consequences related to that charge. Simple possession of an unregistered weapon, or one the defendant is not allowed to possess, is a less serious charge but still carries potential jail time. It's very important for your lawyer to assess the situation and show the court exactly what occurred with that weapon, and why.

Family cases, including domestic violence and *ex parte* protective orders, happen every day. Child abuse and child endangerment are on the rise. If you are charged with this type of crime, it's very important that you obtain the services of a knowledgeable attorney immediately. Forensic work and experts are the name of the game in these situations. For example, I often see parents charged with the death of a child where the state or federal government alleges the baby died from forceful shaking; i.e., "shaken baby syndrome". Many factors, such as bloodshot eyes, may play a part in determining if an assault occurred. It's important that your lawyer get on those issues right away. If your lawyer is not aware of how to handle these cases, it can be very detrimental to the outcome of your case.

Juvenile Crimes

Juvenile cases are becoming a mainstay of our courts. Every county in Maryland has a Juvenile Court which dwells within the county's Circuit Court. However, Juvenile Court is a separate branch which does not intermingle with Circuit Court and is not usually handled by the same state's attorney. Some of the smaller counties that don't have enough court personnel do use the same state's attorney.

I've seen many cases where kids 15, 16, and 17 years old are being charged as adults. It's important for your lawyer to determine if a "reverse waiver" should be filed. It is much better for a person to be adjudicated by a Juvenile Court instead of the adult system. In most cases, the juvenile court system loses all jurisdiction after defendants turn 21.

The whole purpose of Juvenile Court is to try and get treatment and resolve the case without imprisonment. But, there are juvenile detention centers throughout the state, and they often come into play. It's imperative to have a lawyer who understands the juvenile system and how it interacts with the adult system.

5

Overview of the Entire Process

The Investigation Begins

Criminal investigations and charges originate several ways in Maryland. One of the most common is when a citizen files a complaint directly with a police officer. For example, if two people get into a fight at a bar, the police are called, and one of the people may wish to charge the other with assault.

In domestic assaults where family members get into an argument at home, police respond to a call and enter the house. This entry is justified not with a warrant but with "exigent circumstances", meaning the police have probable cause to look into a disturbance and see if everyone is okay. The police then interview the people involved and determine whether criminal charges will be filed. If the police decline to charge, then it is up to the people involved to charge via a commissioner. Police often decline to charge for any "on scene" incident and simply advise going to the commissioner at the local District Court.

Police and Commissioners

Commissioners are judicial officers appointed to initiate criminal charges and issue declarations, such as protective orders and peace orders. If a person declines to press charges against another, that does not mean the police will not make an arrest and charge an individual. In a domestic violence situation, the person making the allegations often does not want the other person arrested once the anger subsides. But the police often do, based on the theory that if a crime has been committed, it's their duty to make an arrest and file a criminal charge.

The law indicates that if a police officer sees a misdemeanor or felony occurring, they are absolutely obligated to make an arrest and begin the criminal process. If a police officer has reasonable suspicion or probable cause that a misdemeanor or felony occurred in the past, then they also have an obligation to file criminal charges or make an arrest. Usually, past-felony investigations are reserved for detectives and administrative investigators.

When a person wants to file criminal charges against someone, they go to see a commissioner who will determine whether probable cause exists for that charge to be filed. For example, if an aggrieved victim goes to a commissioner and claims that an aggressor committed a crime against her, that commissioner must make an assessment to determine if, based on the circumstances presented, that a crime *may* have occurred.

It's not the commissioner's job to show that a crime actually occurred beyond a reasonable doubt. She is a not a judge nor a jury, but merely a scribe in some ways. A commissioner looks at the facts, assessing the person's credibility and determining whether or not the elements of a crime have been met. If so, the commissioner may issue a summons, a warrant, or a charging document in the District Court.

A complainant or victim must write out a statement of facts about the alleged crime and how it occurred. The commissioner will make her determination based on those written facts. Those written facts represent what has alleged to have occurred, and they become evidence to be used later by a criminal defendant's attorney.

In the United States, it is very easy for anyone to go to a commissioner or the police and make up an allegation. It really isn't the commissioner or the police officer's duty to make absolutely sure that the charges are true or false. They are not there to judge as to whether or not the crime actually occurred. They are there to push the allegation into the process of the criminal judicial system.

People who get charged are often upset and angry because they feel as if someone has accused them falsely, and they don't understand the process. They say, "How the hell could this happen? How could someone simply make up something about me and obtain criminal charges?" But while it is easy for someone to make up facts and try to procure a criminal charge, it is very difficult for a person to make the allegations stick if they are false. There are many ways to prove the crime didn't occur.

Grand Juries

The most common method of charging a person with a crime is through a police officer or a commissioner. However, another method uses a grand jury. A grand jury consists of 24 people who will meet in a jury room in the Circuit Court to determine whether a crime may have occurred.

The grand jury room is a sanctum in the sense that a defendant is usually not allowed to be there or be involved, and it is almost entirely run by the prosecutor's office. The government's office will present evidence to the grand jury, usually from the detective or police officer who has knowledge of the crime, and most of the time the grand jury will indict.

You may have heard the saying, "You can indict a ham sandwich." That is very true in the sense that the only evidence presented is from the state or federal prosecutor, and grand juries will usually go along with it. After the grand jury indicts, the process moves on to becoming a case.

A "Criminal Information" Charge

A less common charging document is the "criminal information form". Usually this occurs when criminal charges are filed in the Circuit Court (as opposed to the lower District Court), and the state's attorney's office decides to file criminal charges directly against the defendant. This is a tool that state's attorneys use to get around various defense strategies such as the preliminary hearing, which we will discuss next.

Remember: Almost all criminal charges start in the District Court. So, when a police officer or individual charges someone with a crime, the charges are facilitated through the District Court system. Maryland has "tied together" every District Court in the state. The Circuit Court has the ability to use the same system, but to a lesser degree.

Preliminary Hearings

Nearly every case charged in Maryland starts out in District Court. Even a homicide charge or very serious rape charge starts in the District Court. If a defendant is charged with a felony, then the defendant has an absolute right to a preliminary hearing. A preliminary hearing is a process where a District Court judge will listen to evidence presented by the state's attorney's office to determine whether there is enough evidence for the case to continue to the Circuit Court. In other words, the judge must determine whether the allegations could have occurred.

What is the real purpose of a preliminary hearing, and does it do any good? The answer is unequivocally *yes*. I'll give you two examples.

Suppose you live in a small town in Maryland. You grew up in a situation where the local sheriff didn't like your family or had some problem with you individually. The sheriff has harassed you for a long time, and then he charges you with false crimes for personal reasons. Who can stop him?

The preliminary hearing is designed to prevent abuses of police power and careless use of state authority. If there is a probability or even a hint of evidence that an incident could not have occurred, then the District Court judge at the preliminary hearing should dismiss the charges.

Here is another example. I had a case in western Maryland where a defendant was charged with very serious drug distribution charges. The drugs involved were worth hundreds of thousands of dollars. The state had not yet indicted, so we had a full preliminary hearing. Remember that at the preliminary hearing, the state's attorney's office must present evidence, but the defendant cannot present evidence nor testify. However, her attorney can cross-examine the state's witnesses to determine whether there is probable cause that a crime was committed.

In this particular situation, the state presented a senior police officer who had investigated the charge. The officer testified that he had recovered a large amount of narcotics in the defendant's home. The officer spent a considerable amount of time talking about how it was discovered and what the result was. Finally, the state was obligated to present the fact that the alleged narcotics were actually a controlled dangerous substance prohibited by the state of Maryland. In other words, they had to show lab results that proved the drugs were illegal.

After a lengthy cross-examination about how and where this occurred, I asked a few simple questions about the type of drugs. I analyzed the lab results and noticed the lab report said all the narcotics were heroin. But the officer had testified that the drugs recovered were cocaine. Because this officer categorized the drugs differently from the lab result, we achieved a complete dismissal of the felony charges!

That example is rather simple, but there are many others. I often handle domestic violence cases where the state has charged the defendant with first- and second-degree assault. When a person is charged with multiple counts in District Court and some of them are felonies, only those felonies are subject to the preliminary hearing review.

The difference between first-degree and second-degree assault in Maryland is very important. In simple terms, for the state to prove the elements of first-degree assault, the state must show that it was a very serious assault. Usually a weapon is involved, or some sort of choking which puts the victim close to paralysis or death. Second-degree assault in Maryland is simply an unlawful touching, which can be serious but usually is not life-threatening.

This particular defendant was charged with first-degree assault and, after cross-examining the police officer, I showed that there was no serious possibility of death, even though some strangulation had occurred. Based on that, the felony first-degree assault charge was dismissed.

In these instances of multiple counts which include felonies, the case stays in District Court if the felonies are dismissed at the preliminary hearing. If the hearing finds probable cause, then the case and all its "tag along" misdemeanors will be moved to the Circuit Court.

The "criminal information" method of charging someone is rare, but it gives the state the ability to have the case put directly to the Circuit Court to get more leverage. A very common strategy of the state's attorney's office is to simply indict the individual prior to the preliminary hearing if it believes the defendant may have a chance of getting rid of the felonies. That puts the state in a situation where they have more leverage at the Circuit Court, because the felonies are still alive and the defendant must deal with all the charges.

A defendant and her lawyer need to determine whether or not the case has a chance of staying in the District Court. If it does not, and it proceeds to the Circuit Court, the lawyer needs to understand what strategies can be used. To avoid unpleasant surprises for the client, lawyers need to know about the judges' and prosecutors' habits in certain cases, and also have a deep understanding of each charge and element..

6

What Happens after a Summons or Warrant is Issued, and How Does the Bail Process Work?

Many times, a criminal defendant is not even aware that she has been charged in a matter. Often, the first time she becomes aware of the problem is when she is arrested by the police or receives a summons in the mail indicating that she has a trial date.

A commissioner usually determines whether summons or warrant will be issued. The charging officer and sometimes a state's attorney also play a role. When a complainant describes the alleged severity of the circumstances to the commissioner's office, certain types of cases almost always require a warrant; murder or homicide, a felony sex matter, and child pornography are a few examples.

When the warrant is issued, it is given to the local police department and the "warrant squads" will attempt to serve the defendant. Sometimes they come in the middle of the night, and other times they make routine stops at the house to lock the person up.

I always advise people that if they receive a call from a detective or police officer indicating there is a warrant or that they need to come to the station, please be aware that you will be arrested and put in jail. You need to have your attorney contact them immediately to determine what the status is and how it can be handled. If there is a warrant, it is usually more advantageous to have your lawyer schedule a time to turn yourself in to the arresting officer or detective. That way, you can have all your ducks in a row as far as bail and timing your ability to get out of jail.

A warrant is a declaration order from the state directing a police officer to arrest and take a person into custody. The defendant is taken to a charging center, such as "central booking" in Baltimore. Being arrested is a scary proposition. Many people who find out they have a warrant contact my office, and they are scared to death. They want to know if everything will be okay. Unfortunately, in that situation, the arrest and booking *must* occur. But most people find it comforting to know they have a lawyer in their corner, and they appreciate it when I set up a time for them to turn themselves in so that we can time the arrest and the booking process in a reasonable manner.

Typically, I speak to the arresting officer or the detective and make a deal where the person will turn themselves in at a specific time. I usually do it early in the morning so we can try to get them out hours later. It's important to understand the booking process in a scenario with a warrant. Often, we can get someone turned in, booked, and out within several hours. It simply depends upon the jurisdiction and the crimes alleged.

If a summons is issued, then you don't need to worry about being locked up. The commissioner has deemed the offense not worthy of a warrant, and the court issues you a summons demanding you appear in the District Court to face charges. But a summons doesn't necessarily make the case less serious. It is extremely important to have a lawyer during this period to help you navigate the process.

After you are put in handcuffs, you are taken to the booking department. You may sit there for a short time or maybe a long one, depending on how busy the station is. Once you are booked (which includes fingerprinting and photographing), then other information is obtained from you. In Maryland, each defendant has the right to be seen by a commissioner for a bail review within 24 hours. Usually, that happens shortly after the arrest. In Baltimore Central Booking, it can take two days or more.

A commissioner gathers information from you, assesses the charges, and determines whether bail is appropriate. The commissioner can deny bail, issue a surety bond (which means that an insurance company is involved in posting the bail), issue a high or low bail, or a cash bail. Commissioners in some cases can allow property to be posted in lieu of bail.

Up until a couple years ago, the so-called mini-hearing in front of a commissioner was usually done with just the commissioner and the defendant. It was deemed of little consequence. However, I and many other lawyers believe this step can be very important concerning whether or not bail is given. Recently, lawyers have been allowed to attend these mini-hearings with the commissioner. I think it's helpful in many circumstances.

However, because these hearings may occur at any time of the day or night, it's difficult for a private lawyer to attend. The public defender's office allows lawyers to attend these hearings and get paid through the state so that a person at least has someone they can ask about the process.

If the commissioner sets a bail, the defendant may post bail immediately and walk out of the detention center. That is why it is so important to have the bondsman or the bail bond agency ready to proceed before you are locked up. If the commissioner sets a reasonable bail and you have a bondsman available, the bondsman will usually do the legwork and post bail. They get paid a fee for doing so. Generally, the fee is 10% of the bail, but I have seen a wide range of costs over the years. The bondsman's cost of insurance is usually about 4%, and anything they make over that is profit.

If all goes well, then the defendant should be out within a few hours. However, there are many circumstances where the commissioner will deny bail or set a very high bail. The defendant has the legal right to wait to see a District Court judge, either later that day or the next. They will not be released until that occurs, unless they post bail in the amount set by the commissioner.

At this point, caution is merited, because if you take a chance on getting a better deal with a judge and you strike out, then you may be stuck for quite a while. You're playing with fire if you don't know the ropes and the jurisdiction. It takes a very experienced attorney to know what the chances are for a defendant to receive a bail from a District Court judge if bail was denied by a commissioner or set very high. Many times, people want to take a chance and try to get the bail reduced because the commissioner set it high. Sometimes that turns out to be a mistake, because the District Court judge denies bail. Then all bets are off as far as the commissioner's recommendation. The judge has denied bail, so the defendant will not be getting out.

If the defendant is charged with a felony and has been denied bail, she has the right to a preliminary hearing if requested within ten days. Generally, a defendant is stuck in jail unless she can convince the District Court judge at the preliminary hearing to issue a bail. This is rare, because judges are sitting that day for the preliminary hearing and not any bail review. However, a good lawyer will try to craft a scenario where that can occur if prior bail has been denied. A lawyer can also request that an additional bail review or a *habeas corpus* be heard. (*Habeas corpus* means "bring the body to the court" because it is being held illegally).

Attempts to get the defendant out of jail prior to trial are often futile because of the nature of the charges. The facts of the case and the defendant's background (such as prior criminal history) as well as the nature of the alleged crime will influence that determination. Flight risk, public protection, and a determination if the defendant will show up are what the judge is pondering. Technically, under the Constitution, a defendant deserves a bail release—but not always.

From my experience working with criminal defendants, the bail scenario is one of the most difficult things to determine. The Maryland bail industry has very strong connections to the Maryland General Assembly, and bail bondsmen get paid for their services. The legislature allows the bonds to remain high in many circumstances which, in my opinion, are unreasonable. However, in many Maryland counties, they are now lower than they have ever been and in complete contradiction to other counties where they are set high.

It's wise to have an attorney who knows what she is doing in these circumstances. I've seen many situations where clients opt to have a judge make a determination on the bail when they could have walked out on a commissioner's bail, even if it was set high. Defendants who are uneducated about the process of getting out with the commissioner's bail can end up sitting in jail for weeks or months at a time. It's better to have an experienced attorney make that decision.

On the state level, home detention and community detention is possible, but rare. Usually it's simply being released on bail. On the federal level, there is no "bail", and the standard is much higher. In federal court, judges (or sometimes magistrates) determine whether to release the individual into the community or have them monitored through home detention. Monetary bail is usually not applicable. As with the state, pretrial services will make a determination and recommendation to the judge as to whether the individual should be released.

Many people have accused the bail processes of being antiquated. I agree on many levels. The primary purpose of bail is to ensure that the defendant will show up in court later. The other factors to consider are the dangerousness of the defendant to the community, other potential harm to the community, and the defendant's past record, as well as the facts of the case.

Many judges will err on the side of caution when it is a very serious case and hold the defendant without bail or set a very expensive bail. That is why it's important to have a lawyer with you at the bail review process so she can carve out exceptions as to what's being alleged. The judges and commissioners are required to assume that all the facts alleged in the case are correct. It's not a question of guilt or innocence; it's simply a question of whether or not they should be released on pretrial bail.

7
More about Grand Juries

Grand juries have always been the basis of fascination for TV shows and stories about how people are charged with crimes. "Anyone can indict a ham sandwich" may be true, but it's a little more complicated than that. There are two basic types of juries in our criminal justice system. A petit jury is the one you see in a courtroom where six to twelve people vote on criminal and civil cases. A grand jury is completely different. It is a tool used by the state's attorney's office or the Department of Justice to charge people or sometimes corporations.

The federal system and the state system are similar. Both consist of up to 24 people. Bringing forth an indictment or a criminal charge usually requires two-thirds or three-quarters of the grand jury, depending on the jurisdiction.

To understand what a grand jury does, we need to look inside the mind of a prosecuting attorney. While many indictments are strictly routine, with people charged on a routine basis every week, many are high-profile cases. In some circumstances, a prosecutor may not want to actually file a charge or charges themselves but will leave it to a grand jury to make that determination. It's usually because of a political decision or a high-profile scenario.

Grand juries are highly secretive. If you are selected to be a juror in a grand jury, you must keep everything that occurs within the room a secret. Defense attorneys and their clients are generally not allowed in the grand jury room. The secrecy allows for people to freely speak their minds (testify) and for prosecutors to build cases.

Sometimes it takes weeks or months to build a case. Others occur in minutes. Grand jurors are appointed to the grand jury for a day or sometimes longer. In the latter case, it's usually because the prosecuting agency is building a case against a defendant and needs time to gather evidence and present it, usually through subpoenas or testimony. There are strict state and federal laws about trying to pierce the grand jury veil. In other words, it is illegal for attorneys as well as citizens to disclose any information presented.

Typically, the prosecuting attorney presents evidence to the grand jury. The evidence usually comes from a police officer or other person who has information regarding the alleged crime. There are no hearsay rules, and it is very relaxed, unlike a regular court of law. The prosecuting attorney will question the witnesses and present information to the grand jury.

At the conclusion of the prosecutor's case, the grand jury will vote on whether to return an indictment. An indictment is simply a raising of hands and voting on whether to prosecute. If the grand jury decides to prosecute, then an indictment is signed, sealed, and delivered to the clerk's office of the court.

Earlier, I discussed why people have the right to a preliminary hearing when charged with a felony; that is, the right to have a judicial officer review the facts and determine there is no hanky-panky going on with the prosecutor's office or the police, and to ensure that the government has enough evidence to go forward.

The same is true with the grand jury. The legal theory is that a grand jury is an independent body that can review the facts as applied to law and make sure the government is not playing hanky-panky regarding any decision to prosecute. That is why some prosecuting attorneys like to have grand juries present an indictment, because it absolves the attorney of any blame for being over-zealous in charging a defendant. They simply say that it was up to the grand jury.

Just because a grand jury returns an indictment doesn't mean it's legally sound. There are many circumstances where a grand jury returns an indictment based on evidence that is less than convincing. In rare circumstances, I have filed a motion to ask the court to allow the grand jury proceedings to be recorded so we can get a transcript. This is done because we want to find out if the prosecuting attorney presented evidence properly, and that the grand jury was not misled or told something that can't be proven.

No exaggerations are allowed, and misleading evidence is the basis for a defective indictment and dismissal.

If it can be shown that the evidence presented was untrue, then the defendant may have a motion to dismiss the indictment and also to use the misleading evidence to impugn the government's case. In any high-profile case, it is a normal and standard *modus operandi* to record the grand jury if the defense knows ahead of time that they are meeting.

If a person is indicted, they will not have the right to a preliminary hearing, and District Court proceedings are not involved. From a jurisdiction standpoint, the Circuit Court of the county where the crime was committed immediately has proper jurisdiction, and the case will proceed in the Circuit Court forthwith. Many times, the defendant will have already been charged in the District Court when an indictment is handed down, and jurisdiction is immediately removed from the District Court to the Circuit Court.

8

What Is an Arraignment on the State and Federal Levels?

On the state level, an arraignment is pretty simple. The defendant is required to come to court before the judge who usually advises the defendant in detail of her constitutional rights, and the charges against the defendant are usually read in open court. Sometimes the judge will advise on procedural matters, too. The defendant is advised to have an attorney enter their appearance, and that she could lose certain rights if she does not do so immediately. These are called "use it or lose it rights".

Many courts will allow or require the defendant to enter a plea of not guilty, guilty, or no contest (*nolo contendere*). The latter is very similar to a "not guilty" plea.

Bail Bonds

On the state level, by the time a defendant gets to the Circuit Court for arraignment, the bail and release have already been addressed by a commissioner and a judge. However, there are times when the defendant is still in jail, has been indicted, and is standing before the judge at the Circuit Court for the first time to enter a plea. Wise attorneys will use that opportunity for a bail review if the court allows them to.

If the defendant is still incarcerated and the judge allows the defense attorney to present a bail review, the judge must determine the following items: whether the defendant is a danger to the community, the defendant's criminal record, the defendant's ties to the community (such as how long she has lived there and whether she has family nearby), whether the defendant is employed in the community and for how long, and whether the defendant has any history of failure to appear in court (FTA).

If the judge decides that a bail is proper, then she will determine whether the defendant is released on her own recognizance (ROR). That generally means released with the promise that you will report for trial and not commit any other crimes before then. Judges and commissioners usually release defendants on recognizance if it is a minor case.

If a judge requires the defendant to post a bond or bail, the defendant must post money with the court in order to be released pending completion of the case. The court can require cash bond or a surety bond. If the bond is "cash only", then the defendant must post that amount with the court. Once the case is complete, the money is refunded less any fees the court may have. Usually there are little or no court fees.

If the court allows a surety bond, a bondsman or bail company deposits a percentage of the bond with the court via a "promise to pay bond", a contract that the bondsman will pay the balance of the bond if the defendant does not appear in court and cannot be located. The defendant needs to then pay the bondsman a portion of the bond for their services.

A court can also issue other conditions to protect the community. For example, the court may require the defendant to have no contact with witnesses, not use of drugs or alcohol, not associate with any other defendants involved with the case, not commit any new crimes or have any new arrest, not associate with known criminals, not possess any firearms, and not travel outside the county or the state. If the court determines the defendant violated any of these conditions, the court may rescind the ROR or bond and hold the defendant in jail pending trial.

I have recommended to judges on many occasions that if the court is reluctant to release a defendant on ROR or a regular bail, then they should be able to carve out a supervised release, such as home detention. The court can place the defendant in a supervised release program or on pretrial supervision, which is similar to probation. The defendant may have to report to a probation or other supervising officer to comply with the terms and conditions after they are released prior to trial.

In most jurisdictions, the defendant must appear for arraignment. However, there are some jurisdictions such as Baltimore County Circuit Court or Arundel County Circuit Court where, if a criminal defense lawyer enters their appearance, then the arraignment is waived. The reason is that if an attorney enters on behalf of the defendant, it is deemed that the defendant is being advised properly of the law and the charges. The prosecuting attorney will then forward any charging documents and related evidence to the defense attorney.

There are many other counties in the state, such as Howard County, Carroll County, Baltimore County, and Harford County where the defendant must appear for a preliminary conversation with the court and the state's attorney's office regarding the nature and potential for trial in the case. In these jurisdictions, the arraignment can be very helpful, because you can get a head start as to what the state's attorney is looking for in the case, as well as an actual recommendation or plea offer. Many times, the plea offer is just a starting a point, and I usually do not recommend a defendant immediately take it; however, it gives us an idea where the state's case is.

In many jurisdictions, an arraignment is looked upon as a *pro forma* requirement. Many state's attorneys send clerks to work with the court and defendant regarding the arraignment. The most important function of the court is to advise the defendant of how important it is to get an attorney in that situation, even if it's a public defender, so they can get enough information about the arraignment.

On the federal level, arraignments can be used for many things. Sometimes they resemble the state arraignment, except that the court will determine whether to hold the defendant. The "community release option" is always the first option of the federal courts. However, there are times when people are dangerous to the community or pose such a serious threat that they are held without release. Sometimes subsequent arraignments occur to further address particular issues in a case.

After the Arraignment

What happens after the arraignment? If the defendant is released, then the case proceeds as normal. Sometimes trial dates and motion dates are picked at the arraignment. The trial judge wants to know if there are any motions that are likely to occur so he can schedule them.

After an arraignment, I usually file something called an "omnibus motion". (See Appendix B.) These are the "use it or lose it" motions. I formulate my motions to reflect all the possibilities that may eventually be raised for a defendant in the District or Circuit Court. If you look at the motions in the Appendix, you will see that I've covered just about every possible motion that needs to be raised. If motions are not raised properly, then you lose your right to raise them later in the case.

Despite the fact we file these motions, not all of these issues are litigated. Often, the facts of the case do not even require them. However, motions such as discovery requests, grand jury transfer request, motions to dismiss, Fourth Amendment suppression issues, and speedy trial motions could be very instrumental to a successful outcome.

What happens after the defendant is arraigned and gets a trial date depends on the jurisdiction. Between the time of the arraignment and the trial date, there is usually a "discovery" period where your lawyer should be conducting an investigation, obtaining statements from witnesses, obtaining information from police agencies and the state's attorney, and sometimes negotiating with the state's attorney's office. It is not a time for idle hands. It is a time for earnest efforts so the defendant can benefit from everything that is discovered. Only a couple of counties in Maryland use an online electronic filing system, but most of the counties now use email and other electronic methods to fulfill discovery for the defendant's attorneys.

Generally, state's attorney's offices must provide the defense with any exculpatory information; that is, anything that can help their case. Nothing can be held back. The state must provide every last bit of such evidence. One of the main differences between the state and federal courts is that discovery is handled differently. In federal court, a contractual agreement must be signed. On a state level, most discovery evidence is automatic and must be provided to the defense.

9

What's the Difference between a Criminal Traffic Charge and a Civil Traffic Citation?

There are hundreds of possible traffic offenses, some which are purely civil and others which are combinations of civil and criminal. All these offenses are found under the Maryland Transportation Article. (See Appendix C for a complete list.)

Traffic offenses involve any kind of "transportation". They are not limited to cars and motorcycles. They include bicycles, mopeds, boats, and anything that has a motorized engine and operates on the public (and sometimes private) streets.

Civil traffic offenses are non-jailable and non-criminal. For example, if you get a speeding ticket and are found guilty, the penalties are usually a fine and/or points on your license. Most traffic cases carry no criminal penalties; but if you receive too many civil citations and receive too many points, then you could be charged administratively with the accumulation of points via the Officer of Administrative Hearings. The state oversees your license and penalizes you when you have too many infractions.

But, some civil traffic offenses are simultaneously criminal offenses, which can be confusing for defendants. Maryland's DWI laws are an excellent example. Here, a DWI is both a traffic offense *and* a criminal offense. If found guilty, you could receive points and administrative sanctions, and your driver's license can be taken away or suspended. But those are all civil penalties. A DWI could also result in jail time—the criminal penalty.

DWIs are not the only traffic offense that carry a mix of civil and criminal penalties. For a complete list, see Appendix C. Plus, criminal offenses can be charged alongside traffic offenses. The results of an adjudicated traffic or criminal case are either guilty, not guilty, probation before judgement (PBJ), Stet, or dismissal. See Chapter 17 for a full explanation of these results.

10
Jury Trials Versus Judge Trials— Which One Do I Choose?

Should you have your case tried by a jury, or should you allow the trial judge to hear the case and determine your guilt or innocence? This is one of the most important strategy decisions a defendant needs to make if charged with a crime in Maryland or on the federal level.

Each county in Maryland has at least one District Court. Some counties have more than one, such as Baltimore County, Arundel County, Prince George's County, and Montgomery County. Jury trials are not allowed in District Court, only trial by judge.

In Maryland, District Court judges are appointed to ten-year terms by the "appointment secretary" in the governor's cabinet. They do not run for election. Judges in the District Court generally hear misdemeanor cases, but they also hear some very serious cases which include jail time as a penalty. Most people think of the District Court as a traffic court or the "people's court"; but in reality, District Court judges handle domestic violence, assaults, thefts, DWIs, traffic/criminal matters, and even some fourth-degree sex offenses.

Directly above the District Courts are the Circuit Courts. These are the "trial courts" where defendants may have a jury trial. In Maryland, you have the right to a jury trial if you face a criminal charge punishable by imprisonment for 90 days or more. If you are in a District Court, you can tell the judge you want to "pray" a jury trial, and the case will be removed from the District Court to the Circuit Court. Depending upon the county, it may take months for your jury trial to happen, but sometimes it happens sooner. Either way, you will be given a summons to appear in the Circuit Court.

So, let me tell you what I think about when deciding whether you should have a judge trial or a jury trial. As in every case, it depends upon the jurisdiction, the judge, and the circumstances of the case. Generally, I advise defendants that if the totality of their case hinges on police officer testimony as to guilt or innocence, then seek a jury trial. Why? Because although we have unbelievably great judges in this state, it is a very difficult burden to put on a judge to find that a police officer has "lied" or misrepresented themselves in a case.

Our court systems are made up of "players". Everybody plays a role. For example, the state's attorney's office is usually located in the same building as the judges' chambers, but the public defender's office is generally not. This creates an unbalanced system. Practically speaking, many state's attorney's offices must be near the clerk of the court and the judges' chambers because of the nature of prosecution. However, I've often argued that it gives the state's attorney's office undue and quick access that many public defenders and defense attorneys do not have.

When you look at the longevity of a career in the judicial system, it's inevitable that people in close proximity will become friends and acquaintances, and routinely exchange information. I'm not saying that anyone in our judicial system is not doing their best or lacks integrity. But I am arguing that the prosecution's preferential proximity is inequitable.

Judges tend to see police officers over and over again because police officers make multiple arrests over the years. Judges and state's attorneys become friendly with police agencies and police officers. Consequently, it can become difficult for judges and judicial personnel to tell a police officer he or she did something wrong. This is not always the case, because I often see judges admonish police officers for doing something wrong, but it depends on the circumstances. So, I advise that it may be difficult to win a case that requires a judge to tell a police officer that she did something incorrectly.

However, if there is a *technical* argument about whether a crime occurred, I often recommend requesting a judge trial rather than a jury trial. For example, I have argued in front of judges that a certain law does not apply to a set of facts in a case. Judges have gone to law school. Judges usually have a lengthy legal career prior to sitting on the bench, and the integrity of most judges in this state and across the country is impeccable. Therefore, I recommend to defendants in a "legal argument" scenario that we make use of a judge's knowledge and objectivity.

I'll give you an example. I had a case not long ago where a person was charged with a sexual offense. In Maryland, there are several sexual offenses codified in statutes. Each statute has different elements and facts that must be established by the government. It can get very technical. I argued in front of a judge that the state could not and did not prove its case regarding the elements of a particular sex offense based upon what was heard and seen. The judge agreed and dismissed the charge. That may not have happened with a jury, because not all jurors are inclined to consider the technicalities—only the result.

Let's be honest here. Some jurisdictions are better suited than others to hear certain types of cases. Juries reflect the local population and the moral and social status of a community. I advise defendants to seek jury trials when their fellow citizens may be more inclined to understand and appreciate the sensitivity of their situation.

For example, Baltimore citizens are extremely sensitive to the actions of the Baltimore City Police. Many lawyers use that to their advantage by having a jury trial in Baltimore City when there is a concern about police actions. On the other hand, more rural counties show a solid preference for "law and order".

There is no firm set of rules about whether a defendant should opt for a judge trial or a trial by jury. But a good defense lawyer can offer insight about these basic principles in a specific case or jurisdiction. Every defendant should discuss these aspects of the case with their lawyer to get the best result possible. It could mean the difference between a win and a loss!

11
The Defendant's Best Friend: The Fourth Amendment

I will never forget how amazed and fascinated I was when, as a law student, I first read the Fourth Amendment of the United States Constitution. Its bold statement gets right to the heart of fighting tyranny and restraining the government.

> *"The right of the people to be secure in their persons, houses, papers, and effects, against unreasonable searches and seizures shall not be violated, and no warrants shall issue, but upon probable cause, supported by oath or affirmation, and particular described in a place to be searched, and the persons or things to be seized."*

Those words hit the government right between the eyes. Our founders had the foresight to understand that governments, police departments, and other agencies tend to want to control the populace for their own purposes. The main method they use to implement that control is "search and seizure". This technique has been used by tyrannical governments for centuries, and our founders knew it.

Fourth Amendment discussions usually focus on a search by the police. There are many situations where the Fourth Amendment does not apply because the government is not involved. Our Bill of Rights mostly applies to the government. When law enforcement is involved, citizens have an "expectation of privacy" afforded by the Fourth Amendment. I explain to my clients that the Fourth Amendment has two main provisions. First, it limits and regulates the seizure of a person; and second, it limits and regulates seizure of property.

Let's first looks at the seizure of a person. It happens almost every minute in Maryland. Seizure means an arrest or detention. There have been many Supreme Court and state cases that discuss and define what "seizure" actually means and to what circumstances it applies.

Generally, two elements must be present to constitute a seizure of a person. First, there must be some showing that the police prevented a person from leaving or going about their business according to their own free will. Was the person put in handcuffs? Were weapons used to prevent the person from leaving the immediate area? Did the police use forceful or aggressive language? Was there physical contact by the police, or any kind of indication of authority? Did the police intimidate or bully? All these factors play a part in establishing whether the police prevented a person from leaving and thereby rendered them arrested, stopped, or seized.

This issue has been litigated countless times in state courts, administrative courts, and the Supreme Court of the United States. I've often argued to courts that different people react differently to police and authority. Police and investigators are experts at using authority to get what they want. Consider a person who has never had contact with the police in any serious situation where they are suspected or accused of a crime. That person will usually be scared, and will therefore want to cooperate. Police use that fear to get the result they want! The issue in these circumstances is whether the person had the ability to leave.

Piggybacking on the determination of an improper seizure of a person is the issue of continued detention and questioning without giving Miranda rights. *Miranda v. Arizona* was a 1966 Supreme Court case that established a requirement for police personnel to advise the accused about certain fundamental rights.

> "You have the right to remain silent. Anything you say can and will be used against you in a court of law. You have the right to an attorney. If you cannot afford an attorney, one will be provided for you. Do you understand the rights I have just read to you? With these rights in mind, do you wish to speak to me?"

I see many situations where police officers intimidated a person to get them to talk about a situation, even when the police did not explicitly exert their authority to require the person to stay in the area. In other words, the police play the game of arguing they never arrested nor detained the defendant, and therefore Miranda was not required. I have often argued successfully that the mere presence of a police officer who requests a person do a certain act or discuss a certain subject can be influential and can create a situation of unreasonable detention and search. The officer says, "No, I didn't detain. It was a simply a conversation where the defendant was free to leave anytime". But the reality is that because of officers' body language, appearance, physical presence, and other police techniques, a defendant may feel intimidated. And therefore, I believe Miranda should apply!

I've handled many cases involving traffic stops where police officers in Maryland pulled drivers off the road and, instead of simply approaching the driver and asking for a license and registration, they would play games. After asking for the license and registration, they would engage the driver in a discussion about general, unimportant things.

During the conversation, officers would scrutinize the driver and the contents of the vehicle. That by itself is okay, and it is what a good police officer should do. But these officers drew out the conversation, and thus the vehicle stop, a long, long time.

They asked questions such as "Where have you been", "Where are you going", and "What is your agenda for the night"? They would discuss the driver's personal life. They would take it even further, asking, "Do you have any drugs or contraband in the car?" The driver, who was simply pulled over for speeding, finds herself answering questions that are clearly outside the scope of the stop. Then comes the inevitable question: "Can we search your car?"

Some officers will say (or insinuate) that they can hold the driver there until they call a canine unit. So now, through a simple traffic stop, this officer has cornered the driver into allowing them to search the vehicle! Guess what the police officer testifies to in court? "Judge, she gave full voluntary consent to search the vehicle without any kind of coercion from me. We were just talking, and this was a voluntary, consensual search." Bull!

I've successfully argued to the court on many occasions that this scenario is an unreasonable detention and unreasonable seizure. Most of the people will not simply tell an officer something like, "Hey, officer—shut up! I don't have time to talk to you. Go run my tags and information and get my license back to me as quickly as possible." That is because most citizens are polite to an officer, but also because of the police intimidation factor.

Many times, police will continue to engage the driver and find out that there are drugs in the vehicle or that some other criminal activity had taken place, where they would normally have no probable cause or reasonable suspicion that a crime had taken place. This clearly is an "extension" of a reasonable traffic stop. A police officer's duty is to simply stop the vehicle, gather license information, run the tags, and issue a citation.

If, during the reasonable time it takes the officer to do that, they notice some other crime is happening, then they have reasonable suspicion or probable cause to continue the investigation. The police officer can ask a driver or passenger to exit the vehicle, but the officer must continue with the stop diligently.

The point is that in these situations, police officers have tried to get around the Fourth Amendment. It is very important your lawyer understands the basic elements of the case law regarding the Fourth Amendment to make applicable arguments for you.

The second basic element regarding seizure of a person is that the defendant must submit to the authority of the police officer. In other words, an officer who tries to assert authority during a search is not in violation of the Fourth Amendment if the party does not submit. For example, if you are walking down the street and a police officer yells at to you to stop, but you run away, then the Fourth Amendment does not apply, and a seizure has not occurred.

One of the most powerful provisions of the Fourth Amendment is the request for a warrant. Generally, the government must have a warrant for an arrest (or a search and seizure) unless certain exceptions apply. There are quite a few exceptions.

For example, if probable cause is present and a police officer has a reasonable belief that a suspect has committed a crime prior to the arrest, then the officer can arrest without a warrant. An officer can also arrest a person to prevent their escape or to preserve evidence that a crime occurred.

One of the most common exceptions police use to get around the Fourth Amendment is something called "exigent circumstances". An exigent circumstance is an emergency where a police officer must act immediately to save life or property, and has no time to get a warrant. The courts have said that imminent, serious emergencies are clear exceptions to the warrant requirement. To make the circumstance exigent, probable cause must be present, and the courts have said that "reasonable" grounds must exist, too.

There are thousands of cases serving as precedents about which circumstances or facts are relevant to arguments about the Fourth Amendment. In my Fourth Amendment arguments, I always use the "reasonableness" factor. The courts have consistently said that under the Fourth Amendment, searches and seizures must be "reasonable". No excessive force may be used, and reasonableness is the ultimate measure of constitutionality.

When I analyze the facts of a criminal case, I start with the Fourth Amendment. This is true whether it's a DWI stop, a drug investigation, or any serious, criminal matter. In every case, I ask, "Is the seizure reasonable? Is it reasonable from the government's standpoint, or the defendant's standpoint?" The courts have tried to balance the degree of intrusion with a person's right to privacy, and also with the government's need to provide for the safety of the general public, and the needs of police. The totality of the circumstances must always be considered.

This is the ultimate battleground between the government and individual liberties. A good defense attorney will strike back and argue vehemently against any state or federal government search if there is an unreasonable aspect. Defense lawyers must stand their ground and prevent the government from crossing the line. There really is no one else in our society who can do that!

A defendant who has not completed law school and has not practiced law does not understand the nuances of these cases. There are thousands of precedent-setting cases to understand before one can get a grip on how the Fourth Amendment works and whether it's applicable. I always start and end my cases on the presumption that the police have violated the Fourth Amendment. Many of my cases hinge on suppressing evidence gained through Fourth Amendment violations by the state and the government.

The ultimate penalty in any constitutional argument is the "exclusionary" law. The Supreme Court has said that if the government violates the Fourth Amendment in any provision, then the exclusionary rule applies. This rule means that if any evidence is obtained illegally, it cannot be used to prosecute the defendant. The founders were brilliant in leveling the playing field with that ultimate penalty to the government. Truly, it backs up the belief that a free society would rather 100 guilty people go free than one innocent person be convicted due to excessive prosecution from the government.

You may wonder how this applies to you and your case. Out of the thousands of cases I've handled, approximately 75% involve an analysis of the Fourth Amendment. Every ordinary traffic stop where there is seizure of drugs or other contraband involves an exclusionary rule analysis. The Fourth Amendment pertains to every home search warrant and every other intrusion by the government to obtain and seize evidence to prosecute someone.

To successfully enforce the exclusionary rule, motions must be filed immediately. They are called "use or lose it" motions, and if the court is not made aware by your defense lawyer of her intent to suppress evidence, then that argument could be waived. This is not applicable under rules for Maryland's District Court, but it does apply in the Circuit Courts and most definitely applies in the federal District Court. The government must be put on notice that you are making an argument for suppression.

12
Sex Crimes

Sex offense cases are one of the primary types of cases my firm handles. We are a leading law firm in Maryland in terms of the great number of these cases we deal with, and our ability to effectively handle them. I don't care what any other lawyer says about these cases. They are the most difficult, humbling, exciting, and revealing cases in criminal law. Sex offense cases bring out the best and worst in people. In many ways, sex is still a mystery in our society, and it can be life-altering to try to understand why people lie, cheat, and break the law in this arena.

Let's start by acknowledging that sex offenses have been around since the beginning of time. Our society likes to believe the fallacy that national and state legislation has led to the successful prosecution of sex offenders. In some cases, it has. But truthfully, the court dockets are full of these cases, proof that not much of a deterrent exists.

One of the major problems with labeling someone as a "sex offender" is that it's an oversimplification of many complex phenomena. There are so many different layers and elements of sex offenses that they don't all fit into one simple category. However, most people are afraid to take the time to separate the different classes of offenders.

Since the early 1990s, Congress and most state legislatures (including Maryland) have created a policy process which tries to reduce and prevent sexual crimes via sex offender registration and very stern sentences of jail time. Sex crime is a significant public health issue, so the government has adopted many psychological philosophies about how these offenses can be reduced.

The government's main plan of attack focuses on recidivism: the likelihood that an offender will repeat the crime. In 1994, the federal government enacted the *Jacob Wetterling Crimes Against*

Children and Sexually Violent Offender Registration Act. It helped law enforcement "track" sex offenders to reduce the likelihood that they would act again. Prosecutors are very sensitive as to whether the defendant will repeat the crime, and this idea is the foundation of the sex offender registry and why it exists in every state. The purpose of the registry is to notify people about sex offenders so people can "keep an eye on them".

Psychiatrists, psychologists, and leading doctors have theorized that sex offenders can never change. In other words, a sex offender is usually doomed to repeat his or her sexually predatory behavior and therefore must be confined in jails or watched closely so they can't repeat their behavior. That's what the government believes, but I disagree.

Another significant law was passed in 1996: *Megan's Law*. This law amended the Wetterling Act by requiring all states to establish systems for making registry information available to the public through methods of community notification. (Hence the Maryland sex offender registry we all know and love today.) Megan's Law made photographs, names, and addresses of registered sex offenders available to the public via the Internet and other forms of notification. The theory is that this helps cut down on any type of recidivism.

In 2006, Congress was still looking for a way to classify sex offenders, and it passed the *Adam Walsh Child and Safety Protection Act*. This law piggybacked on prior, similar laws. It created a tiered registry system and further streamlined the process of tracking and notifying about sex offenders. This statute further reclassified how state sex offender registration systems were to be set up. Because of this law, Maryland now has a three-tier system. The Act got into specifics about which crimes would appear in each tier. Generally, Tier 1 is a mandatory 15-year registration, Tier 2 is a 25-year mandatory registration, and Tier 3 is a lifetime requirement.

Congress wanted to classify, categorize, and keep a watchful eye on these offenders. Again, Congress believed that since many offenders are prone to recidivism, they can only be watched or confined, as opposed to counseled and treated.

Next, I will briefly discuss each major sex crime as classified in Maryland. If you are facing sex crime charges, this will help you know where you stand. Generally, federal crimes resemble these categories from the Maryland criminal code.

Rape in the First Degree

Generally, a person may not engage in vaginal intercourse with another by force or threat of force without consent of the other person. To convict someone of first-degree rape, prosecutors must show that either a dangerous weapon was used or displayed, or some physical object the victim could reasonably believe was dangerous. Suffocation, strangulation, disfigurement, or an intent to inflict serious physical injury to a victim is also a means. Threatening or placing a victim in serious, imminent fear is a requirement.

Generally, rape in the first degree is exactly what it sounds like: A person (male) forces a female to engage in sexual intercourse. Many of these cases are situations where a person broke into a home, committed a rape, and left. In that situation, DNA, follicles, semen, and other forensic materials come into play. Often, these cases are affected by the requirement in Maryland that all felony conviction defendants must give a sample of DNA. All these DNA samples are placed in a central registry where they are used for future reference. They are very useful in solving old crimes.

Many times, the key issue in a rape scenario is whether penetration actually happened. The prosecutor attempts to show that penetration did occur, based on evidence from a doctor, safe nurse, or other medical professional. The other issue is whether the victim consented to the penetration, and it can be much more difficult to find conclusive evidence about that.

One of my cases illustrates this point. A male physician was engaged in an intimate relationship with a female who also worked at the hospital. These two people knew each other for several years before dating. They engaged in sexual contact with each other, and generally called each other boyfriend and girlfriend.

However, as discovered during the trial, these two had a very sordid history. The relationship was very rocky, both emotionally and physically. The alleged victim engaged in sadomasochism. Merriam Webster's Dictionary defines sadomasochism as "sexual behavior that involves getting pleasure from causing or feeling pain". These two people engaged in sexual contact where each of them would inflict pain on the other in various sexual acts. Both people were extremely involved in sadomasochism, and they were members of various websites and groups focused on these behaviors. They would perform sexual acts such as intercourse, oral sex, and other sexual manipulation while inflicting pain on each other. This included tying up each other, beating each other, spanking each other with leather belts, inflicting emotional and psychological pain, and withholding and ordering certain sexual acts from each other. I think you get the picture.

This case started when the female told the defendant that she no longer wanted to be with him. This seemed to be something they both did to each other, constantly. She would express this to the defendant, and then he would do the same, and then they always got back together. This went on for years.

One day, the defendant was so despondent about her leaving him that he seriously contemplated suicide. Alone at his home, he held a gun to his head. Then he put it back down. Then he started to pull the gun back up to put it to his head, but the gun accidently fired and shot his hand. A bullet went through his hand and he began to bleed profusely. He panicked.

He called her and asked her to take him to the hospital. She steadfastly refused and told him to go to the hospital himself. He then drove to her home, and this is where the criminal scenario begins.

The facts showed that he entered the home bleeding profusely and asked her again to take him to the hospital. She refused. Then, despite the fact that he was wounded, they began to engage in sexual sadomasochism.

The defendant stated that the victim agreed to engage in sexual intercourse. The victim alleged it was simply rape with no consent. The defendant tied her up and penetrated her vagina with his penis. He also engaged in certain other S&M acts with her during that time. The defendant testified that, over the last month or two when the couple had intercourse, she would not allow him to ejaculate. As revenge, he ejaculated in her on this occasion, and he stated this infuriated her. She was then untied.

A dispute as to what happened next was put on the record in front of the jury. The victim alleged that the defendant began to physically abuse her and kept her captive in the house for hours. She alleged that she tried to run out of the house naked to the neighbor's house and, because they were in a rural area, the houses were quite far apart.

He chased her. A video from the neighbor showed both of them running across the neighbor's yard naked, with him chasing her until he finally caught her and tackled her on the driveway. The defendant alleged that this was part of their sadomasochism behavior.

She indicated on the stand that after a couple hours of allegedly pleading for her life, she convinced the defendant to let her go. After hours of struggle and alleged kidnapping, the defendant finally left to go to the hospital. The victim then called the police, and the defendant was arrested several miles from her home.

During the trial, I cross-examined the victim. I brought to light the many sadomasochistic acts the two had engaged in previously. The alleged victim was hesitant to discuss these acts, but I extracted in front of the jury all the details of what these two had engaged in. Ultimately, the jury did not believe her on all counts, and the defendant was found not guilty on most of them.

The case started on a Monday and ended on a Friday night. The jury went out to decide the case at 5:00 p.m., and I convinced the judge to allow the jury to stay there until the decision was made at 3 in the morning. I don't think the bailiffs were happy about staying until 3:00 a.m.

You can see how there can be a dispute about whether there was consent or a lack of consent in certain situations.

Another scenario I see very often involves two people who engage in sex after meeting at a local bar and both drinking a great amount of alcohol. In the morning, they have conflicting stories.

The alleged victim doesn't remember the sexual contact but subsequently learns it happened. Often, the victim believes that since she doesn't remember, it must not have been consensual, so she calls the police.

To complicate it even more, often a current boyfriend or spouse learns of the sexual encounter and confronts the person, who then states that she doesn't remember, and didn't consent, and so it must have been rape. This happens so often with young people when alcohol or drugs are involved. There is a lesson here.

I represented a group of young men in a local college fraternity who were all accused of raping an 18-year-old freshman from Towson University. The alleged victim went to a frat party where she became somewhat drunk and, for some reason, began to engage in sexual activities in the basement pool room with five of the frat members. Everyone was intoxicated, and she engaged with these young men for over an hour.

The issue became about whether the victim so intoxicated that she could not properly form consent, and whether the young men should have engaged with her under those circumstances. From a moral viewpoint, the answer is *no*. But morality does not always equate to the law. The victim alleged that she was taken advantage of and was so intoxicated that she had no idea what was happening. She told the police she was raped, and each one of the males was subject to serious prosecution if charged.

Then, a video showed up. The video clearly showed the young woman engaging with the males in sexual acts for a long time. She was conversing, laughing, and clearly demonstrated on video that she was not so intoxicated that she could not have formed consent.

Consequently, I convinced the state's attorney's office they could not prove their case, and the young men were not charged. But it was a sad state of affairs for everyone involved, including the young woman. Ask yourself why she made this allegation. As with many sex cases, there are so many possible factors that no one really knows. But I do know this much: Once an alleged victim tells their story many times, they feel "boxed in". In other words, they must then live up to the story. Many actually believe they were wronged. And many times, they were!

Rape in the Second Degree

A person may not engage in vaginal intercourse with another by force or threat of force without the consent of the other. The primary difference between first-degree and second-degree rape is the lack of a weapon.

This statute revolves around consent as well. I often see a situation where a person is charged with having intercourse and the alleged victim cannot consent because they are mentally defective. This statute also holds that if the victim is under the age of 14 and the person performing the act is at least four years older than the victim, then second-degree rape occurred.

If you look closely at the age requirement, then two people in a case like this may have had contact when they were in high school. In other words, you could have a senior student who is 19 and a younger student under the age of 14 who engage in the same social spheres and end up having sexual relations. In that situation, the defendant is technically committing a crime simply because of the age requirement. I've often advocated that there should be what I call "the high school exception".

Sexual Offense in the First Degree

This statute prohibits a person from engaging in a "sexual act" with another by force or the threat of force without the consent of the alleged victim. To meet the requirements of the statute, the defendant must employ or display a dangerous weapon or physical object that the victim reasonably believes is a weapon, or suffocate, strangle, disfigure, or inflict serious physical injury to the victim, or threaten to. In many ways, this statute mirrors the rape statute, except there does not need to be vaginal intercourse. It deals with other acts which are sexual in nature.

Sexual Offense in the Second Degree

This statute prohibits a person from engaging in a "sexual act" with another by force or threat of force without the consent of the other. If the alleged victim is mentally defective, then there is a crime. This statute also has an age requirement about the victim being under the age of 14 and the person performing the sexual act (it doesn't have to be intercourse) being at least four years older than the victim. I see many cases where the state's attorney's office will charge second-degree rape as well as sexual offense in the second degree if the case involves a statutory age difference.

Sexual Offense in the Third Degree

This statute prohibits a person from engaging in "sexual contact" with another without the consent of the other while employing or displaying a dangerous weapon or other physical object that the victim reasonably believes is a dangerous weapon. A person may not suffocate, strangle, disfigure, or inflict serious physical injury to the victim, or threaten to.

The big difference between this sexual offense and the other sexual offenses is that the sexual level is "sexual contact". Sexual *act* and sexual *contact* have been defined differently. Generally, a sexual act is more serious than sexual contact. Sexual contact tends to denote a sexual touching.

Sexual Offense in the Fourth Degree

This statute prohibits a person in a position of authority (such as a teacher, babysitter, or family member) who is at least 21 years of age from engaging in sexual contact without the consent of the other, or engaging in a sexual act with a person who is 14 or 15 years old when the person performing the sexual act is four years older than the victim. This is a slight variation of the other sexual offenses, and it has other meanings, too.

The big difference between fourth-degree sex offense and the other sex offenses is that there is an opportunity to keep people off the Maryland sex offender registry if they are convicted of fourth-degree sex offense. Sex offense in the fourth degree may be heard in District Court as a misdemeanor. However, it is often heard in Circuit Court because it is tacked on to felony charges. A judge may allow a person to receive probation before judgement, and then the registry can be avoided. The state's attorney's office often uses this charge when dealing with alleged touching or contact with a minor.

Sodomy

Sodomy is defined as "anal or oral copulation with a member of the same or opposite sex". Many of Maryland's sexual laws are antiquated. Our legislature should reform these antiquated laws as quickly as possible. Maryland's sodomy law criminalizes all kinds of non-vaginal sex, including consensual sex between opposite-sex couples and consensual sex between same-sex couples.

But realistically, the state has not prosecuted consensual, non-commercial sex since the late 1990s. However, I saw sodomy charges tacked onto several other kinds of sex offense charges not that long ago. It's unlikely we'll see these prosecutions anymore except under a special circumstance.

Unnatural or Perverted Sexual Practices

Maryland's unnatural or perverted sexual practice statutes are also clearly antiquated. They prohibit a person from taking the sexual organ of another person (or animal) in the mouth. A person may not place their own sexual organ in the mouth of another person (or animal) and/or commit another unnatural, perverted sexual practice with another person or animal. If convicted, a person is guilty of misdemeanor subjected to imprisonment not exceeding ten years.

I understand the prohibition of sexual practice with animals. However, this antiquated law regarding oral sex with people needs to come off the books. Very seldom do we see charges under these statutes, but I do see them once in a while.

Sexual Solicitation of a Minor

I see these crimes often in the Baltimore metropolitan area but not so much in the rural counties of Maryland. This statute prohibits a person from knowingly soliciting a minor to engage in sexual contact, sexual acts, or rape. These cases focus on the person's *intent*. A person found guilty of this felony could be subject to a prison term not exceeding ten years or a fine not exceeding $25,000, or both.

With the advent of the Internet, we are seeing more and more contact between adults and under-aged people for sexual purposes. Most police agencies have established undercover detectives who go online and have discussions with people who are engaged in this type of contact. The popular TV series *To Catch a Predator* showed exactly what these detectives do.

But these cases can be very difficult for the state to prove. Typically, you'll have an undercover detective posing as either a male or female 14-year-old and trying to entice an adult into soliciting them or meeting them for sex. The undercover detective tries to get the other person to send naked photographs, face photographs, or photos with other identifying features. The detective also tries to get them to engage in sexually provocative conversation. Once that happens, a meeting is set up at a house or a public location such as a McDonald's. Once the person arrives at the parking lot, the officers spring into action and arrest him. The chat transcripts are then used as evidence against the defendant.

I have used the defense of entrapment and also other defenses to try to help people in this situation. Many defendants say to me, "Jim, how can I be convicted of any type of solicitation when all I did was drive to the place and not get out of the car?" This may be true, but the main focus of the statute is to determine the defendant's *intent*. Did he bring alcohol or drugs with him? Did he bring any type of toy or object to try to entice the young person? Did he bring condoms? The judge of jury considers all these things—the totality of the situation—when making a determination.

Indecent Exposure

This is an evolving statute which needs the attention of the Maryland legislature. Many people are charged with this crime and are potentially subject to serious consequences when, in my opinion, the acts don't constitute a crime.

Generally, indecent exposure is the intentional act of exposing one's genitals or private parts in a public place (or even in a private place, sometimes). Conviction of this offense does not require sex offender registration, but there have been many attempts to change that, and it's quite possible it might happen in the future.

The problem with this crime is that it covers many different scenarios but is not well-defined by case law or even the statute itself. I'll give you a couple of examples. Not long ago, I represented a college student who was charged with indecent exposure. This student was drinking one night with his friends in the college dorm. Because he had been a student on campus for a couple of years, he knew the local security personnel and knew where they would and would not be at any given time.

As the evening progressed, several of his friends moved from the dorm room to the outside area. It was dark out. The college student was joking around with his friends outside and, from a distance, he "mooned" them. A police officer saw this from a great distance and came to the scene. The student was charged with indecent exposure and subsequently charged with violating the student code of conduct. Needless to say, this caused him many problems.

The case law relating to indecent exposure is somewhat vague and antiquated. The question in this situation was whether the intentional exposure of his buttocks in a public place constituted indecent exposure. I created a privacy defense. My argument was that under the circumstances this was not a public place. The fact that it was dark and only his friends were there created an expectation of privacy, and hence this was not a violation of the law.

The District Court judge agreed with me, and the defendant was found not guilty. However, I see many of these cases where the exposure of buttocks, breasts, or even partial genitalia are prosecuted. I argued that many buttocks are exposed on beaches by scanty swimwear such as thongs. The buttocks are completely exposed except for the one portion that is covered. The police officer never testified that he could see the student's genitals, so I argued that the behavior was not outside the norm of society. The problem the state had with this statute is that its original intent was to simply prevent people from exposing themselves in public. Common sense should prevail.

In another case, I represented a well-established couple in their 50s who were married and went out on a date night. The husband and wife both worked very hard, and they were celebrating the fact that their children were now out of the house. They had become "empty nesters". This night was a celebration and a chance to reconnect their relationship. Both were great people and had very successful careers helping others.

They went to a bar and restaurant. On the way home, they pulled over in a secluded area on the side of the road to "reconnect." They started kissing and making out in the car. They were giggling, and the husband teased his wife by opening her blouse and exposing her breasts. The wife did the same by touching the man's genitals and exposing them.

Now remember, this was a dark, secluded road. Yes, there were homes around, but no one was outside. Then, a police officer arrived, apparently responding to a call from a neighbor who noticed the car parked at the end of the street. The police officer approached them quietly, and he saw the woman's breasts.

Unbelievably, even after discussing the situation with these people and realizing they were two responsible adults who were just out having a little fun, the police officer charged them with indecent exposure. This caused them major problems with their employment and the community. The husband had a governmental clearance. After talking with the state's attorney, I got the case dismissed. But you can see how police discretion plays a huge role in these cases. Sometimes a little common sense goes a long way.

Most municipalities such as Baltimore have local statutes prohibiting public urination. I've seen situations where people were out late at night in the city, at bars or restaurant locations such as Federal Hill or Fell's Point, and they urinated in an alley or secluded place. Sometimes police officers, instead of issuing a citation for public urination, will issue an indecent exposure charge. The two are very different, and you can see there is much room for abuse in that scenario.

13
Child Pornography—Remain Calm!

My office handles a tremendous number of state and federal child pornography cases. I feel like a renegade in this area of the law. When I first started to handle CP and sex offense cases, I delved into what makes many of these alleged perpetrators tick. I found many of these people have no criminal background at all. They might be hard workers, productive members of society, and even great parents and grandparents. Sometimes depression controls them, and sometimes drugs and alcohol contribute, too. My cases taught me that our government and our society try to categorize these people with a one-size-fits-all approach.

Nothing could be further from the truth. I found the investigations resembled the McCarthy-era witch hunts. When you're charged for these crimes, then you're "red" (as communists were called back then) and guilty as sin. But there are as many false accusations in sex offense and CP cases as there are actual crimes. Maybe more. One size does *not* fit all, and the government does not understand that.

This area of the law is exploding. It's the fastest rising crime in this country! I have immersed myself into understanding how and why these laws are violated, and how I can most effectively represent my clients. To better understand the nature of these laws and crimes, we will be primarily addressing state laws.

Let's start with obscenity. Under the criminal code, obscene matter is prohibited by several statutes which have a deeply rooted foundation in this country. They prohibit possession of pictures, drawings, photographs, films, video, or even written material that meets certain criteria.

Most of us are aware that possessing, manufacturing, or distributing of images or video of underage children is illegal. An interesting new series of cases addresses fake imagery. Fake imagery can be drawings, cartoons, anime, and even a combination of film and fake imagery. Fundamentally, obscenity laws are designed to protect the moral standards of the local community. These laws have been attacked on several bases, most importantly the free speech rights under the First Amendment.

Let's look at the meat and potatoes of these laws. The possession, manufacture, and distribution of child pornography is addressed under Section 11-207 and 11-208 of the Maryland Code. Let's start with simple possession of child pornography.

Section 11-208 prohibits a person from knowingly and intentionally possessing a film, videotape, photograph, or visual representation of a person under the age of 16 engaged in certain acts (mainly sexual conduct), in a state of sexual excitement, or engaged in sadomasochistic abuse. The penalty for this violation is not more than five years in jail or a $2,500 fine. A subsequent violation of this statute could entail a sentence of not more than ten years or a fine of $10,000.

Almost all the child pornography cases I run across now involve the Internet. Very seldom are there cases where the origin of the material is from something other than the Internet, such as magazines.

In an attempt to push some of the burden back onto the state, the legislature created affirmative defenses to this charge. If a person takes reasonable steps to destroy any images or video, or reports the matter to a law enforcement agency, then they are deemed not guilty of this statute.

Section 11-207 prohibits inducing, soliciting, or knowingly allowing a minor to engage as a subject of obscene material (child pornography), and visual representations or performances depicting a minor as subjected to sadomasochistic abuse or sexual conduct. This statute includes photographs, films, video, computer transmissions, advertisements, and solicitations, and also distribution or intent to distribute any of these visual representations. The penalty for this crime is a potential ten years in prison or a fine not to exceed $25,000 (or both). Subsequent violations receive up to 25 years in prison or a fine not to exceed $50,000 (or both).

On the federal level, if a person is convicted of any type of distribution of child pornography, there is a mandatory five-year federal prison sentence without any discretion by the judge. There is no federal parole. If the defendant is simply charged with possession on a federal level, although there is no mandatory jail sentence, there is a higher likelihood that some jail time will occur. If you are dealing with manufacturing or production of child pornography on the federal level, there is also a mandatory sentence.

When I first started representing people in these types of cases, the offenses struck me as sad and something that reflected a mental illness or major psychological problem with the person charged. But over the years, I've learned that many people who are charged with this type of crime do not actually engage in any of this type of sex offense. In other words, most people assume if a defendant possess child pornography, then they are the kind of person who would engage in a sexually deviant act with a real child. The statistics do not bear that out. In fact, although there is recidivism in people who commit actual sexual acts with children, there is less likelihood of recidivism regarding child pornography users.

I find in this day and age that many people, including young males (and some females) as well as older people tend to lose themselves in the world of computer-based pornography. If a person is prone to depression or any other illness where they isolate themselves, then they may be very susceptible to the addiction of pornography. These people will spend hours and days at a time on a computer looking at these images and fantasizing as an escape from real life.

Many tend to categorize and list the different types of pornography, including the child pornography. I call these people collectors. It's almost as if their entire life is focused on the computer when they are not working or when they have any "down time".

When I started to see patterns of these users, I asked myself, "Why does this happen, and what are we really dealing with here"? After hiring many experts and discussing these situations with doctors, psychologists, and other therapists, I have come to certain conclusions.

I have read a tremendous amount of medical and psychological material on this subject. Much of the medical evidence shows that users begin with simple, legal pornography. It became apparent, after discussing their history and pathology with most of these defendants, that a dependency on pornographic sexual acts became an addiction.

Let's face it. There are some people who are simply attracted to underage children sexually. Those people are prone to these attractions, and they need serious therapy and help. I am not talking them. What I'm talking about is people who may have no real propensity to actually be involved with or attracted to children. They simply think or believe they want to view this material because their brain has been trained to do so.

We need to ask ourselves, "Why would these people look at child pornography, and why would they use the computer to masturbate while watching it?" A long time ago, I discovered a website called YourBrainOnPorn.com. I was referred to it by an expert while handling a sex offense case. I recommend that anyone who is charged with a sex offense or has an issue with pornography read that site in its entirety. It is especially helpful to spouses and family members. If you have teenage children, it's imperative to discuss these issues with them.

The site argues that pornography can be addictive. Science now says (although it's disputed by some in the medical field) that when a male looks at pornography and sees sexual acts occurring, it can actually change the structure of his brain. This site has many articles and publications arguing that brain structure and functional connectivity is associated with pornography consumption.

It argues that spending great amounts of time watching pornography correlates with a reduction of "grey matter" and sections of the brain's reward circuitry involved in motivation and decision making. Reduced grey matter in this reward-related region means fewer nerve connections. Fewer nerve connections lead to sluggish reward activity or a non-pleasure response, often called desensitization. The nerve connections between the reward circuit and the pre-frontal cortex degrade with increased porn watching. In short, the site argues, there is evidence of an association between porn use and impaired impulse control.

These studies argue vehemently that the more pornography that is consumed by the user, the less dopamine is secreted during any sexual arousal. The basic argument is that when a male views images of sexual acts in pornography, the brain itself cannot really determine the difference between real life and images on the screen. In other words, the male will get excited and get an erection, and the brain releases dopamine. Of course, the male knows the images on the screen are video, but the mechanics of the brain and the central nervous system respond as if it were real. The user is, in fact, training and creating new pathways in the brain as to how he has sex. The brain "learns" how to have sex.

However, the more pornography is consumed, the less dopamine is released. Doctors argue that people will consume more and more pornography to try to become stimulated, although the user may not understand what they are essentially trying to do is to get that dopamine release. The problem is that the brain will not release constant dopamine when watching the same sexual act over and over, hour after hour.

A normal male brain is not used to seeing thousands of naked images of people in real life. The stimulus of constantly watching these naked images on the screen creates a desensitizing effect. Eventually the mechanism wears out, and less dopamine is secreted. This may cause dysfunctions such as inability to maintain erections, the degradation of interpersonal communication skills, an inability to have a close sexual relationship, depression, the inability to function in a positive manner in society, and a lack of self-esteem.

It's clearly shown in studies that this overuse of pornography may cause people to retreat within themselves and not feel confident enough with the opposite sex or in society in general. Thus, we see many young people (and older) resorting to pornography as a preferred method of stimuli as opposed to the real thing: a sexual and emotional relationship with another person.

So, you may be asking yourself, "What the heck does this have to do with *child* pornography?" All the studies I've read and the experts I've talked to lead me to conclude that pornography is a highly addictive product. Many people watch pornography with very little effect on their sexual performance, relationships, and libido. But there are also many who become highly addicted.

Legal hard-core and soft-core pornography production is one of the biggest industries in the world. It's more common than breathing in and out! Many people will deny watching any type of porn, but SOMEONE is definitely watching it. Porn consumers spend *billions* of dollars. Porn is the most popular past-time on the Internet. And science shows it is harmful. By watching normal sexual acts in abundance, the brain eventually gets used to it and becomes "dumbed down". The dopamine and the reward system will not respond as much because of the overuse.

This is where the porn industry is brilliant. It understands that there must be other acts and other deviant scenarios to arouse or catch the viewer's interest as time goes on. Sadly, if you look at some of these sites, you will see there are hundreds of crazy sexual acts that are shown. You can simply click on some to view the different and more deviant ones. The idea is to keep the viewer interested and keep that dopamine flowing!

A person who looks at pornography for years becomes dopamine-deficient and bored, and he goes looking for that next adventure. He is looking for something to get his attention and release more dopamine. Strangely enough, it's not always about the sexual attraction of a particular act. Doctors have argued that sometimes it's the deviancy or the thrill of a taboo "no-no act" that may get the viewer aroused. Going outside the norm and looking at deviant photographs of people having sex with animals or even with children causes that "no-no" effect and causes the dopamine to be released. So, the user might believe he is attracted to the particular act, but it's really the novelty and newness of the act that drives the dopamine release. That's human nature. It's what keeps the human species surviving: variety.

Now, I am in no way arguing that this is unilaterally true. Obviously, there are different scenarios. In many circumstances, viewers are not interested in *actually* having sex with children—or any other type of deviant acts. They have fallen into a pattern and a depressive state of mind; or, they are looking for scenarios they *think* they are sexually attracted to, but it's only the drive for more dopamine leading them to view deviant acts, including child porn.

This is not an excuse, and I am not offering this as an argument to allow or not prohibit the viewing, possession, or distribution of child pornography. What I am saying is that the science shows there is a progressively addictive behavior in people who may have looked at or even collected child pornography.

I have handled countless CP cases where great people have simply made mistakes. I've spoken to people of all age groups who say to me, "Jim, I have no idea why I looked at that, or why I even possessed it. It was like I temporarily lost my mind, and I regret it so much." Many of them don't even realize *why* they did what they did; and after they have spoken to a qualified sex therapist, they tend to realize why and how they got themselves in this situation. In fact, many of them abhor the idea of actually having sex with a child; and when they really think about the implications of what this does to children around the world, they become sickened.

Sensitivity and awareness need to be discussed regarding child pornography. Many people who look at child pornography are distanced from the reality of it. They don't think of the image on the screen as an actual person. Our society has become more visual, and we tend to think of what we see on a TV or computer screen as unreal. Consider the news reports of murders and violent acts being committed every single day, all across the country. Unless they take place right in front of us, it can be difficult to perceive them as really happening. So, many defendants I talk to don't even realize or consider that yes, it is in fact a *real child* being abused on the other end of the computer.

Years ago, Congress established the National Center for Missing & Exploited Children. It is a great agency for a great cause, and its sole duty is to report the sexual exploitation of children and try to help the victims. As such, the Center's goal is to list, categorize, and contact every child who has been depicted in any child abuse video or images. Even if these children are on the other side of the world, the Center tries to categorize and become aware of the images they were involved in. And the child porn industry has become a worldwide business.

Prosecutors have argued for years that every time someone views or consumes child pornography, they are promoting the child pornography industry and causing it to grow. I disagree. While viewing child pornography does further the industry and create a situation that is harmful to children, I do not believe that viewing without paying, or obtaining free child pornography, promotes the industry. To understand the worldwide business, you must look at the origins and causes of why these things occur. Many manufacturers of child pornography do it for money, but others do it for many other reasons. Some are people abusing a child close to them, and others are doing it on a larger scale. None of these things are acceptable.

I have argued successfully to federal and state judges that the simple viewing of these images does not cause the promotion of them. If it did, then that same philosophy would have to apply to any other addictive vices in our society. I make the argument about murder. Remember all the magazines that had "true crime" on their covers? They were detective stories about real murders with images of bodies and outlines of bodies in the street. Even the old TV series *Murder, She Wrote* had storylines about killing. My grandmother loved that series. Did it promote murder in our society? I think not.

But there are other arguments I do agree with regarding the actual harm of viewing CP. Imagine you're a person who was abused many years ago, and the images or video are locked on the Internet forever. You must live with that, day-in and day-out. That's a harm that has been perpetrated on the victim. Once those images are released into the public domain, that victim must face their entire life knowing they are out there.

Should a defendant who had nothing to do with the production or the actual, original abuse be made to pay a price years later to this child (maybe now an adult) who was harmed by someone else who put the images or video on the Internet, many years before the defendant viewed them? Should that defendant be made to pay any financial restitution to the victim? That's a difficult question because it deals with the proximity of the act and the harm caused. There is a causal connection between the actual viewing and the harm caused to the victim, but each case may vary.

In state court, there is no mechanism for the victim to receive monetary restitution via the criminal charge. In theory, the victim could sue the defendant (barring any issues about the statute of limitations), but that scenario is highly unlikely. However, in federal court, the issue of restitution is brought up as a matter of course in almost every CP case.

A few years ago, I had a case of national notoriety where a young man was charged in federal court with the distribution of child pornography. To effectively explain this case, I need to first tell you how law enforcement handles these situations.

On the state and federal levels, detectives are usually undercover, trolling the internet for child pornography consumers and abusers. There exist state police, county police, and specialized federal agencies that immerse themselves in technology monitoring and tracking people throughout the state. I've visited the rooms where the monitoring happens, and they look like something out of a nuclear submarine.

Each detective in these rooms is assigned several computers, and they have specialized programs for tracking down the distribution of CP. Most of the time, the case begins when a detective searches for people who might have CP on their hard drives. People who use bit torrent programs allow themselves to be exposed to police investigators to see what they have downloaded. Bit torrent is a content distribution protocol that enables software distribution and peer-to-peer file sharing.

Originally, torrents were for TV shows and music; now they are used for movies, music videos, and any other type of video. A user downloads a bit torrent program on their computer, and millions of other people have, too. Once the user downloads it and requests a protocol to swarm, scatter, and gather the types of files he wants, the content is brought to his computer. Users can simply request pornography or child pornography and let the software get it for them.

This means police can use the system to download these images from the computers of anyone who is on the bit torrent program. If police can download it from your hard drive, they can establish that you have these images on your computer. In the eyes of the law, this may establish distribution and possession.

After police determine that you possess or are distributing CP, they file a subpoena to your cable provider and get the IP address for your computer. Then they obtain your actual, physical address.

Typically, the detectives and the federal agents (called sexual offense units) will show up at a house around 4:30 or 5:00 in the morning when everyone is sleeping, and they take the house by surprise. They enter the house and separate everyone inside. They inspect each computer in the house, one-by-one.

Here is a prime example of how detectives extract confessions. People are scared and embarrassed in front of their family, and it's not hard to get them talking. If detectives can get someone to admit to downloading and possessing the CP on their computer, then nine times out of ten they have a great case after that. The detectives will then run different programs on the computers to see if there is any CP on the hard drive or other devices, and then confiscate them.

Many times, people are not arrested and charged that day, because the computers are taken to a lab where all evidence of the images is extracted. That can take up to one year in some jurisdictions. Others are quite fast.

Back to my federal case! I represented a young man who lived at home with his parents, and he was viewing child pornography. However, this was no ordinary young man. This kid was brilliant about everything to do with computers. He used torrents effectively, but he also got onto the "dark web" where much of the child pornography exists. He retrieved many underground images this way. In fact, by the end of the case, he was teaching federal agents how to access and navigate these sites.

The lab results determined he had over a million images and videos of CP on his computers. This was a really sad case, because he was under 20 years of age and, throughout his young life, he had been bullied and beat up by most of his peers. He was truly a nice and kind young man who worked at a local restaurant part-time while he went to school, but he was unable to fully engage in society or have any social life. When he was younger, he had determined he was gay. But because of the small, rural town he grew up in, he was never able to "come out of the closet". Consequently, he lived a very secretive and secluded life.

He was afraid to tell his parents, and he couldn't reach out to anyone at school because there were no clubs or other avenues for him to talk to anybody about it. Guess what he turned to? He turned to the Internet, and as a young man he began to learn about what he desired by watching regular gay porn. But eventually, he became completely depressed and despondent about life, and he began viewing child pornography.

Eventually he was charged with distribution and possession of CP in federal District Court. My office did a lot of work on that case, and we resolved it in an equitable fashion. He received a sentence that was one of the lowest sentences in quite some time in federal court for this type of charge.

Many lawyers from across the country contacted me to discuss the methodologies I used in this case. Earlier, I discussed how a Maryland statute allows for a person to escape prosecution if they genuinely try to erase or get rid of the image. It all goes back to *mens rea,* meaning "intent". It is absolutely imperative that you have an attorney who knows how these file-sharing systems work, and how to effectively use expert testimony.

For years, prosecutors have argued that distribution occurs when a person is sharing the images from their hard drive to another. The police argue that if they can download the images from your computer, then that is distribution of CP. Federal and state prosecutors agree. But I have vehemently argued this does not by itself prove intent to distribute—and here is why.

The bit torrent programs, which are usually available to download for free, require you to check a box during the set-up, and that checkbox determines whether the program can share your hard drive's content with other users. Many people don't even pay attention to the set-up procedure, and so the sharing is automatically allowed. In that case, the user doesn't even realize they are allowing others to view their content. Many of them just want to look at images and don't give a damn about what happens with the software.

Negligence is not a prerequisite. *Proof* must be established that a reasonable person would have or should have known the images would be shared. Hence, knowledge of the user and their technology skills can play a part in determining intent.

Expert testimony also plays a huge role in making determinations about intent to distribute. Often, the prosecutor is unable to prove intent about was actually viewed, because of the user's search terms. Search terms are an important factor in determining the defendant's state of mind and intent. We have often looked at the search terms the defendant used in the bit torrent program and argued they show no intent to look at actual child pornography. Many of the experts I have used have testified that if a person requests various types of pornography, unintentional and unrequested CP images or video will show up in the large group of images that get downloaded. I've heard this complaint from many people, so always be aware of what you download.

Anyone charged with a sexual offense should be evaluated by a qualified therapist as soon as possible. This is legally desirable, and good for your future mental health. I always have people go for a psychological and drug-and-alcohol screening as well as a sex offense screening. These standardized evaluations can help a judge or state's attorney determine whether someone is a predatory pedophile. They can determine if someone is prone to repeat these actions or was simply caught in the crossfire regarding ambiguous images that were downloaded.

When a person is charged with CP, they realize the seriousness of the situation. They almost always believe that life as they know it is over. But that is not always the case. I have successfully argued many times that the defendant should receive the benefit of probation before judgement; and if that is the case, then they are usually not required to register as a sex offender. To convince a judge of this outcome, it must be found that the defendant is not a harm to the community, and that this was an isolated incident. Other times, I have used "affirmative defense" to defeat the prosecution. These are facts other than those alleged by the prosecutor which, if proven, defeat their case. In other words, we won!

In these cases, many state's attorneys take the position that jail time should automatically apply. I disagree, and I have defended many times without jail time involved. I dislike that many prosecutors will immediately request that my client enter into a plea agreement that includes jail time, or else the prosecution will send the case to the federal system which may require a mandatory five-year sentence. This is total nonsense and, in my opinion, is prosecutorial misconduct. I say to them, "Guess what? We are going to trial!" Quite often, that is enough to call their bluff.

Each CP case is different. Yes, there are many common defenses and issues, but your case needs to be approached in a unique way. You need an attorney who is willing to fight for you and to understand how these proceedings work.

14

The Sex Offender Registry — Do I Need to Fear It?

In sex offense and child porn cases, the primary concern for most people is avoiding the sex offender registry. Maryland is not the first state to enact a modern-day sex offender registry. In the United States, "registration" was first used in the 1930s for repeat criminals and sometimes sex offenders. As a method of driving out people who were believed to be undesirables in a community, it worked. One of the earliest rudimentary state sex offender registration statutes was enacted in California in 1947.

In 1994, Congress passed the *Jacob Wetterling Crimes Against Children and Sexually Violent Offender Registration Act*. The federal act required all states to create registries of offenders convicted of sexually violent offenses or crimes against children, and to establish heightened registration requirements for highly dangerous sex offenders. It further required offenders to verify their addresses annually for ten years, and for sexually violent predators to verify addresses on a quarterly basis for life. States that did not establish registration programs in compliance with the Act's provisions would be subject to a 10% reduction in federal funds.

Most states have since complied. New Jersey was one of the first to implement a sex offender registry and notification law in 1994. Soon after, the Maryland legislature enacted its own registry statute to comply with federal law. Maryland's first sex offender registration occurred in 1995. In recent years, sex crimes committed by repeat offenders have caused many state legislatures, including Maryland's, to enact laws that increase community awareness of these offenders.

State and federal laws require convicted sex offenders to register with local law enforcement and other state agencies. The registrants must supply their addresses and other identifying information such as work, activities, and daily routines. These laws have been enacted in every state.

The theory is that registration allows sex offenders to be more visible to law enforcement and the public, with the aim of increasing awareness. According to this theory, if you know a sex offender lives in your neighborhood, then you can keep an eye on him. By notifying citizens when a registered sex offender is living in their neighborhood, the registry helps people protect their children. The psychological theory behind sex offenses has always been that offenders will offend repeatedly if they are not placed in a controlled environment. Hence, the registry not only notifies people but "keeps an eye" on the offender.

The entire theory from a medical and mental standpoint rests on the fact that many psychologists have espoused the idea that a person is incapable of or unlikely to change from being a sexual predator. In other words, you can't rehabilitate someone with those inclinations, so we need to manage them and make the public aware so people can protect themselves.

I wholeheartedly disagree with this approach. The first problem with the registry is that it classifies all kinds of unrelated things as if they were the same. A true child predator is listed right next to someone who had a crush on a 14-year-old when he was 19 and had consensual sexual relations with her. Lumping these things together is deplorable, and it ruins many lives.

It's very important that your lawyer completely understands who must register and when. Many times, attorneys and judges lack this understanding.

Maryland has classified sex offenses into tiers. The more serious the offense, the higher the tier. Most of these classifications were created to comply with federal requirements. Sex offenders are required to register for at least ten years.

- Tier 1 is a 15-year term (sometimes 10).
- Tier 2 is a 25-year term.
- Tier 3 is a lifetime registration requirement.

Maryland has categorized sex offenders into four different groups.
1. A typical offender.
2. A child sexual offender.
3. A sexually violent offender.
4. A sexually violent predator.

For years, the courts have determined that being placed on the registry was not a "punishment". But recently, courts have realized that the registry *is* a form of punishment, even though it is not jail time.

15

How Lawyers and Clients Can Communicate Effectively

I've spoken to thousands of people whose lives are in peril and whose freedom is at stake. I look in their eyes and see the distress and the angst about what might happen. Most of them are good people who made a mistake or have been accused of something they didn't do. But there are people in this world who are unrepentant and don't care about others, and who are justifiably charged with crimes.

How a lawyer and a client communicate is extremely important. Communication is the key, but it isn't always done effectively! Most lawyers tend to talk "at" clients, and many clients are disgruntled and really don't have much faith in what their lawyer is doing.

The art of communication is one of the most difficult aspects of representing clients. Sometimes clients don't even realize when their lawyer has done something noteworthy or good for them. That's the lawyers fault for not explaining what is happening in detail. Lawyers should not assume that the client understands.

Most clients have no idea what is happening with their case. They only know that *someone* is handling the matter, and they need to show up at different times. They want to know what the outcome will be and what the chances of success are, but the rest can be a blur to them. They are scared. The stress has put them in a daze. They have other issues troubling them. They can't focus properly, because this may be the worst time in their life!

Lawyers need to understand that. It's crisis time for many of these folks, and they deserve to have lawyers treat and represent them properly. Lawyers should bend over backwards to make sure they understand. Let clients know how hard you are fighting for them. If you don't tell them how good you are, they won't know! Of course, a lawyer can never give a client a definite answer about a particular outcome (unless it's an ABA plea), but a lawyer can give a general idea about where the client will end up.

How do lawyers and clients communicate effectively, and what can lawyers do to make it happen? First, the lawyer needs to take control. That doesn't mean that clients aren't responsible as well. Sometimes after going into great detail about a case, explaining how I interpret the facts and the possible outcome, and spending hours educating the client's family on every aspect of the case, I discover no one even remembers what I said!

Of course, clients want to know what the law is all about and how it works. But they sometimes have selective hearing because they want a specific outcome. I advise the young lawyers in my firm to be aware of this. Clients want to know what the final outcome is! Period.

It's similar to going to a doctor and receiving good or bad news about a medical prognosis. The patient might not even remember the details of what the doctor said—only the result or diagnosis. Therefore, it is important to temper what you say to a client. Give a fair and accurate representation of what might and might not happen. No exaggerations, no bluffing, and no pontificating—just a clear, concise description of where they're headed.

It's difficult for an attorney to give a client bad news. When clients are facing jail time, it's the lawyer's job to be direct. It's also the lawyer's job to give a perspective on what can be realistically accomplished, and what can't be.

One of the first things I discuss with clients is who can sit in on the consultation. Sometimes it's good to have friends and family members there, but many times these people have no idea what's going on. Even though they haven't retained me yet, I carefully explain that, as their potential lawyer, I am bound by the laws of ethics and confidentiality. In other words, what they tell me is privileged and confidential; but if they tell me something in front of their friend, the information is not privileged with *their friend*. At least, I'm sure that's what the government would argue if the information was discovered!

Communication with a client in the beginning can be tricky. A lawyer must be allowed to "paint" the conversation the way she needs to. The rules of professional conduct prevent a lawyer from allowing a defendant to lie on the stand. In other words, if a lawyer has a good idea that the client is being dishonest, then the lawyer is duty-bound to not allow that client to promote or testify to false information. In some situations, the lawyer is required notify the court about it.

That is why I make it clear to clients that I don't really want to know what the facts are from *their* perspective right away. What's important is whether the government can prove its case against my client, and not necessarily what kind of case the client can put together. Sometimes, the defendant's case changes and needs to be discussed as matters unfold.

I instruct all the lawyers in my office to make sure there's effective communication through writing, email, and sometimes texting. But there's nothing better than meeting face-to-face with a client, and I insist that mine come into the office every once in a while just to make sure we are on the same page.

If you do something great for a client, tell them about it! Explain to them what happened and what you did for them. Many lawyers make the mistake of doing good work handling a client's case, and then merely informing them of the outcome. Clients want to know what the procedure is and what their lawyer is doing. If they don't know the details of what happened, then that is poor communication and can lead to a bad outcome.

16
If You've Been Charged, Don't Panic!

Yes, I know it's easy for me to say, right? Because I'm the attorney, and you're the one who is charged with the crime. However, I mean what I say. Take a look at how many people are charged in the criminal justice system each year. There are so many police officers from different local and state agencies that it sometimes appears that almost half of society is involved with some sort of administrative or criminal issue.

Although I don't like saying it, I believe most young adults will get into some sort of difficulty with the police. It's just the nature of our society. There are so many police and criminal agencies that *something* is bound to occur, even if it's minor, especially with underage alcohol or controlled substance possession. This is not an excuse, and I'm certainly not telling you, "Don't worry about it" if you or your child have been charged with a crime. But I am saying that if you look at the Maryland docket each day, you will see hundreds of people being charged. Many of these crimes are frivolous, and some do "go away". But that rarely happens on its own without a good lawyer!

There's only an *opportunity* for justice. A highly skilled and well-paid lawyer gives a defendant a much better opportunity for success than a lawyer who does not have much knowledge or expertise. But I've seen many young and talented lawyers make up the difference in experience through hard work and diligence. Judges tend to respect lawyers who do their homework and know what they're talking about.

Judges also tend to respect lawyers that are not necessarily aggressive in their speaking but are aggressive in their forethought and knowing in what direction they want to take the case. Creating success in a criminal case is just that. A lawyer must create it and make it happen.

If you are charged with a crime, it is imperative that you speak with your lawyer as soon as possible. Preserving evidence in a case can sometimes "turn the coin" very quickly. One thing I often come across is video evidence. For example, in a misdemeanor barroom fight or an assault case, the incident might be recorded on local video. However, many merchants "loop" their video so that it's only available for a day or two. If it's not gathered quickly, then that evidence may be gone forever.

Eyewitness and other testimony or evidence is also important. A good lawyer will engage the client and a client's family to help gather this evidence. Gathering witness statements locks witnesses into what they are saying so they can't change their story later. Mapping out where the crime allegedly occurred and how it happened really sheds light on the overall guilt-or-innocence issue.

Many young people who are charged with a crime while in college must deal with the college ethics or peer review committees. Many times, that committee can be harsher than the District or Circuit Court. The entire goal for a person charged with a crime is to effectively handle the charge itself and, if possible, keep the charge off their record. And then, get it expunged!

With more serious cases, that's not always possible, and there may be other goals such as simply staying out of jail. Criminal cases can often be resolved amicably in a way that does not cause future harm to the defendant's career or livelihood. It's like going to a dentist to have your tooth pulled. If you don't have it done, the tooth could get infected and cause even more serious problems. But if taken care of immediately and succinctly, it should not become a major problem.

Good defense lawyers work with local prosecutors to resolve cases before they go to trial. But sometimes, I purposefully avoid contacting a District Court state's attorney so I can surprise them at the trial. A good defense attorney knows that the burden is on the prosecution to make sure all their ducks are in a row on the day of the trial. Why not take advantage of that for your client? A good defense lawyer will be able to pick the case apart and convince the state's attorney they can't get a conviction.

The bottom line is that it's better to obtain the services of an attorney quickly so you can make a solid game plan to effectively handle the charges.

17
What Are the Possible Outcomes of My Criminal Case?

If you are charged with a criminal case in Maryland, it's inevitable that you will end up in the District Court or Circuit Court to have your case adjudicated. The term "adjudicated" means that the case is concluded with some finality. If the case starts out in District Court, you have the absolute right to "pray" a jury trial (meaning the case is transferred to the Circuit Court) or to choose to have the case adjudicated in District Court. If your case starts in Circuit Court, then you have the absolute right to a jury trial (if the possible penalty is more than 90 days in jail) or to have a trial by only a judge.

There are five basic possibilities of how your case can be adjudicated and finalized:
1. Not Guilty Verdict
2. Guilty Verdict or Plea
3. Stet
4. *Nolle Prosequi* (Dismissal)
5. Probation Before Judgement (PBJ)

Not Guilty Verdict

"Not guilty" means the case was tried before a judge or a jury, and that a judge or jury rendered a judgement that you are not guilty of a specific charge, or all charges. As with any case, defendants are sometimes charged with more than one "count". Each count is a "act" or "series of acts". State's attorneys sometimes use multiple counts to bolster their case and try to convince the defendant to "cut a deal" because of the amount of charges against them. Sometimes, the extra counts charged against a defendant will sway them to accept a plea even if some of the counts are a stretch to prove. The prosecutor does it for leverage, pure and simple.

The term "not guilty" means that a trier of fact listened to the case after the government presented their case into evidence and your lawyer had the opportunity to cross-examine witnesses and also present a case on your behalf. The interesting thing about a not-guilty finding in Maryland is that you have the absolute right to have that case expunged. To have it expunged, you must file a petition for expungement. However, that process is not automatic, and there are certain rules and provisions governing it.

Guilty Verdict or Plea

A guilty finding by a judge or jury means you were determined beyond a reasonable doubt to have committed a crime. That guilty finding will go on your record and, if it's a state case, will be listed on the Maryland Judiciary as well as the court records. Most people don't realize that state records are eventually transferred to other state and federal agencies such as the FBI and other governmental gatekeepers.

If you are found guilty by a judge, then she must determine what your sentence will be. Your sentence could include jail or probation, or it could simply include a fine. It could also include a definitive term of incarceration that is totally or partially suspended.

For example, if a judge issues a ten-year sentence to the Department of Corrections in Maryland and suspends all but one year, then nine of those years will not actually include incarceration—unless the defendant screws up on probation. This is typically called a "split sentence".

A judge may use many different components to formulate the sentence and probation. Typically, a sentence will include jail or no jail, probation or no probation, and a fine that is either payable or suspended. A judge may order a person to attend classes, to complete community hours, to attend programs, and to actively participate in other events formulated in the sentence.

Stet

In Latin, the term "stet" means "let it stand". Placing your case in a Stet docket means the state's attorney's office will place your case on the inactive docket for a period of three years. Generally, for a defendant to accept the Stet means he must accept conditions attached to the Stet and not commit any other crimes. Sometimes there may be other conditions required, and they can be in-depth or simple. Let me give you a couple examples of cases I've handled with a Stet.

One example is where the prosecutor believes the case may be very serious, but they have limited evidence to prove their case. So, I try to convince the state to offer a Stet. If I can convince them that I'm right about any particular issue, then it may make them think they can't win. I'll then submit that my client will accept a Stet, and all is well.

A prime reason for the success of this compromise is that it creates the appearance that the State is doing something to protect the general public. Sometimes I will even offer for my client to complete certain classes on abuse intervention, solicitation of prostitution, theft, shoplifting, or other crimes. It's much better to have clients go through the fuss of these requirements than to actually face criminal charges.

As a side note, I have created various psychological and therapy programs with a local counseling center that is very well-known in Maryland. I created these classes for my clients because I used to see them a long time ago in Baltimore, but they no longer existed. So, I created them to give the state's attorney's office and the defendants an opportunity to resolve the case based on the defendant's attending these classes.

Another example of a Stet is a scenario where the state feels they don't have enough evidence to prove their case and, in fact, the case is not very serious. The defendant may agree to certain conditions such as performing community service, staying away from the victim, and receiving psychological counseling. After the defendant completes the programs or tasks, the case will not be prosecuted.

Sometimes I take it a step further. I've had cases where I convinced the state's attorney to Stet the case pending certain conditions to be completed. I've then asked the state's attorney to set the case on a future docket where it can be converted to a *nolle prosequi*, which is Latin for "no longer prosecute." The case can then be expunged immediately.

It's important to know that the state or defendant may reopen the Stet for any reasonable cause whatsoever upon a motion to the judge within 12 months from the date of the adjudication. After one year, and for up to three years, the case can then only be reopened with "good cause". Very seldom do I see Stet cases reopened. It has happened, but generally it's because the defendant has committed an additional crime related to the issue at hand.

Nolle Prosequi (Dismissal)

Sometimes a prosecutor will simply dismiss a case. Usually it's because your lawyer has brought forth arguments prior to trial pointing out to the state that a particular count (or the entire case) cannot be proven. If the prosecutor agrees, then the case goes away. That is why it is so important that your legal team investigate the situation to bring all the facts to the attention of the prosecutor. Remember: Most prosecutors are very busy people, and they simply pick up a file and prosecute it without spending much time on it. That's not always true, but it often is in District Court.

If the case is in Circuit Court, then generally it is a more serious situation. Multiple state's attorneys and even other investigators with the state's attorney's office may pick up the file and handle it. This contrasts with District Court, where they may not even know about the case until a short time before the trial. It is good for your lawyer to point out certain circumstances, then bring them to the attention of the state's attorney so they can decide how to proceed.

Here is an example of a recent case I handled in Anne Arundel County. My defendant was charged as a peeping Tom. He was accused of peeping at an underage girl in a dressing room by using his phone to record her without clothing. The state's attorney's office claimed that he surreptitiously placed the phone on an angle at the bottom of the stall to capture her image on video. The state attempted to prosecute him based on these facts.

My team obtained surveillance video from several cameras at the store. Upon review, I determined that the state would not be able to prove their case. In fact, after carefully reviewing the evidence, I felt they could not prove that he actually recorded any video at all. The state didn't have to actually produce the video. They could have argued that he recorded it and then deleted it. But that's where a forensic expert really comes in handy! I convinced the state to dismiss the case. The defendant was very happy, especially since he escaped the dreaded sex offender registry!

Probation Before Judgement (PBJ)

Probation before judgement is probably the most controversial adjudication method in the state of Maryland, although it's been codified as a statute for many years. Typically, when a defendant is given this sentence, she is first found guilty of the crime or traffic offense. At the sentencing phase, a defendant's lawyer will then ask the judge to "strike" the guilty finding and offer the defendant a PBJ. This means the defendant can then honestly say she has never been convicted of a crime because the guilty finding is stricken, and all that remains is the PBJ verdict. To accept this type of disposition, the defendant must waive their appellate rights, because when the guilty finding is stricken, there is nothing on the record to appeal. After three years, the defendant can apply for an expungement.

It's important for criminal defendants to understand what the limitations are with probation before judgement. I have seen countless situations, especially in the last ten years where criminal defendants who are not U.S. citizens go to court and have their case resolved with this type of adjudication. At first glance, it appears to be great for them, because they can honestly say they have never had a conviction in the state of Maryland. And it is a great disposition in many circumstances. But the problem is that the federal government refuses to cooperate. Remember: There are 49 other states and territories that have other types of dispositions.

For federal immigration purposes, and other federal administrative or employment purposes, probation before judgement is not recognized as a "not guilty" verdict. The federal government, depending on the nature of the crime, may still try to deport a person based upon the severity and potential penalty of incarceration. In other words, if a person has any type of pending immigration issues, they must look at the scenario very carefully. It could affect them in the future.

I've seen many situations where people ask me to file a motion called "*coram nobis*, post-conviction", a procedure to try to have their cases overturned and receive probation before judgement for a crime that carries a lengthy jail time. But the federal government does not recognize PBJ and may still deport the individual. It's a tricky nuance, and your lawyer needs to be well-aware of the possible consequences.

Expungement

The eventual goal in many of these dispositions is expungement. Generally speaking, when a person receives a not-guilty finding, they may file for an expungement immediately. It is not automatically completed; but generally if there is no other crime or aggravating circumstances, it will be expunged.

A guilty finding can be fatal to your future. If the court finds you guilty of a crime, you cannot normally come back later and fix it when you are in a better state of mind. Many people just want to get the case over with. And if they have a guilty finding on their record but no other collateral consequences, they go home and don't worry about it. The problem is, however, that this affects employment, immigration, housing, and many other circumstances in your life.

When I was a young man, if someone was found guilty of a crime, then people did not usually find out about it unless a thorough background check was done. Now, with the advent of computers, that has changed. When a person is found guilty, literally 15 minutes later people on a different continent will know about it. It is a very serious matter, and people should never accept a guilty finding unless there is absolutely no other choice.

A guilty finding can rarely be expunged. I have used techniques such as a *coram nobis* (Latin for "before us") post-conviction, a factual innocence motion, and other petitions to request a modification. But it's better to take care of it at the time of your court case, not years down the road.

You can expunge a Stet after three years, generally. Again, there are no guarantees and, depending on other prior charges you may have, the court will make a determination. The same process occurs with probation before judgement. Generally, the defendant may file for expungement of the case for probation before judgement after three years. Again, whether the case can be expunged depends on whether the defendant has other cases, and the nature of the present one.

Generally, if a criminal defendant intends to sue a police agency or any other governmental entity, the civil statute of limitations is three years. The state does not want to be in a situation where it expunged all records of a case only for the defendant to sue them civilly afterwards. The state would then be caught with their pants down, as they would have no records for defending the case. That is the general idea behind the three-year expungement rule.

18

Maryland's
Justice Reinvestment Act of 2016

In closing, I want to briefly discuss this new law enacted by the Maryland state legislature, because it affects many different crimes. It changes the state's prosecutorial philosophies for certain criminal activities. It represents a schematic shift from policies adopted during the "war on drugs", which many critics indicate has not worked. We've prosecuted millions of people in this country for drug charges, but the success rate is rather low. It is time for something new, and Maryland's Governor and legislature agree.

We've incarcerated more people in the last century than any other country on earth, and the cost increases every year. The goal of the Reinvestment Act is to reduce Maryland's prison population over the next ten years. The legislature believes it will save more than $80 million that could be used on other programs. The Act has steered Maryland towards treatment rather than incarceration for drug use.

Generally speaking, sentences will be lowered on non-marijuana drug possession from up to four years to not more than one year for a first offense, 18 months for a second or third offense, and two to four years for subsequent offenses. The law also provides guidance to the court to direct offenders with substance-abuse disorders into treatment facilities, and it encourages aggressive treatment. Many courts are already handling matters this way, but this policy will "amp up" the preference for treatment instead of jail.

This law makes a notable reduction in penalties for marijuana possession. It eliminates the disparity between crack and powder cocaine as far as who is using it and what the penalties are. This has been a valid complaint for many years, as minorities have received harsher sentences.

Of greatest significance is that this new law eliminates many mandatory minimum sentences for commercial drug offenses except major volume dealers and drug kingpins. It removes the ability of prosecutors to double the sentences for subsequent drug offenders, unless the defendant has been previously convicted of a violent crime. Also, it makes third and subsequent commercial drug offenders eligible for parole after serving 50% of a sentence.

Many notable state's attorneys have complained about these changes because the serious threat of mandatory sentences convinces would-be defendants to cut a deal. But I like it and think it's a much-needed change. Why should prosecutors be given extra tools to bully people into taking deals that include jail time?

This law also modified many of the release policies regarding administrative parole, diminution parole credits, and geriatric parole. It established presumed "parole approval" for certain offenders convicted of drug offenses and misdemeanor property offenses who generally had neither been accused nor convicted of violent offenses. The diminution credits that generally would be taken away in parole violations prior to this law allow offenders to keep some or most of their credits. The new law also ensures that low-level drug offenders get ten days of good-time credits for every 30 days served.

The important thing to remember is that this law changes much of the philosophy and prosecution theories in Maryland. It creates a softer, kinder, and gentler approach for drug offenses and non-violent offenses rather than the harsh mandatory sentences that prevail throughout the system now.

ABOUT THE AUTHOR

James E. Crawford, Jr., was born October 15, 1961, in Baltimore, Maryland. He grew up there, and subsequently Catonsville, and later moved with his family to Ellicott City. Jim graduated from Mount Saint Joseph High School in 1980. He attended Essex Community College and Frostburg State College and received his bachelor of science degree. He played basketball in high school and college.

Jim has always had a passion for politics. He comes from a family that believes service to the community and involvement in politics is a fundamental requirement to be a productive member of society. Jim's political career ranges from being one of the youngest elected state officials in Maryland's history to handling many state, local, and judicial campaigns. From a very young age, he made Baltimore politics a staple in his life. His father, James E. Crawford, Sr., was a practicing lawyer in Baltimore and established a political career as a young man.

Jim used that knowledge and experience to further his own involvement. As a kid, he learned how to run a campaign. As a young man, participated in election picnics, debates, walkarounds, and door-to-door campaigns. He witnessed many political backdoor deals and saw many candidates elected—and some who lost. He became the consummate worker in Baltimore politics, working on City Council races, mayoral races (Don Schaffer being the one of the most notorious), Attorney General races, state Senate races, delegate races, County Executive races, State Central Committee races, and gubernatorial races. In his legal career, he put that knowledge to work for his clients' benefit.

In 1984, Jim became the youngest elected official in Maryland when he was elected to the state's Democratic Central Committee. In 1986, he ran for the Maryland House of Delegates in one of the most notorious races in southwest Baltimore County. He ran against an established political machine and stood on his own against formidable opponents. Since then, he has run and participated in many local, county, and state campaigns. Running campaigns has given him great insight into the practice of law. Jim says, "If you can relate to everyday people on a campaign trail, then you have a winning formula in a courtroom."

Jim earned a master's degree from Baltimore University in 1987. He earned his juris doctorate degree from University of Baltimore School of Law in 1992. He was married in 1991 and now has four children.

After law school, Jim went into private practice and opened a law firm in Baltimore in 1992. As a general practitioner, he handled cases with a focus on criminal law. Over the years, he established himself as a premier practitioner in the state of Maryland. He came to understand that accomplishing his mission of practicing law at a high level would require offering to his community the services he would want if he needed legal representation himself. So, he expanded his firm into the full-service law firm that it is today.

Because he worked for the insurance industry, he had a fantastic head start on understanding civil and criminal litigation. His firm quickly flourished as he worked around the clock to benefit his clients. Now, 13 employees work at the firm, and Jim considers them the best in the state. His office manager, Dawn Basso, has been with him since the beginning. As she likes to say, "That's 27 years of putting up with a relentless lawyer."

Since 1992, Jim has represented thousands of clients in Maryland courtrooms nearly every day of his career, and he has tried thousands of criminal cases in District Court, Circuit Court, and many administrative agencies. His area of practice includes all types of serious criminal law and high-profile litigation. He has an extraordinary record of success in his 26 years of trial experience in federal and state courts throughout Maryland and beyond. He is recognized as one of the most able, tenacious trial lawyers in Maryland. His peers have recognized him as a leader in the legal community for many years.

Jim has always served communities and strived to help those in need. Jim established (as Executive CEO) a Baltimore Charity Group known as "Baltimore Beez". The group feeds people around the holidays and helps other Baltimore charities. Now an executive board member at Mount Saint Joseph High School, he has given countless hours to the school, and his academic program has donated and built a much-needed baseball stadium there.

Since entering private practice, Jim has handled many notable cases that have appeared in the media. His clients range from ordinary citizens to police officers, professional athletes, lawyers, doctors, and politicians. Noteworthy cases Jim has handled include:

Representation of a 17-year old who was accused of rape of a minor. The issue, as Jim saw it, was whether the Maryland should charge the 17-year-old as a juvenile or an adult. Currently, Maryland uses two distinct systems where a defendant is either charged as an adult or a juvenile. Jim has urged the legislature and courts to create a "blended" juvenile system so that the juvenile can be charged as an adult but receive service as a juvenile. Jim was successful in handling that case. The media story was handled by Fox News 45, WBAL Channel DB2.

Representation of a person accused of selling CDS (Controlled Dangerous Substance) in Baltimore by police officers who arrested and subsequently beat him on two occasions. Fox News 45 interviewed Jim, who got the charges against his client dismissed in toto.

Representation of a long-time worker at the Catholic Church accused of sexually molesting a client for years. The client was charged in Baltimore County. Jim successfully negotiated a deal that allowed the defendant to receive parole and get out of jail within a reasonable time. The news story was handled by Fox News 45 of Baltimore.

Representation of a professional basketball player who was charged with several serious crimes. Jim resolved the case with no implications that would affect the player's basketball career.

Representation of a young man who was accused of serious sex offenses in Baltimore County. The charges were so serious that any conviction would have ruined the client's life. After a thorough investigation, and applying current developments regarding the admissibility of forensic evidence, Jim got the case dismissed.

Representation of a young man in Baltimore who was accused of raping and murdering an eight-year-old. The defendant was charged along with two other people. The case made national headlines. After a jury trial lasting a week and a half, Jim's client was acquitted of all charges. The other two defendants were found guilty and given life sentences.

Representation of a man in Maryland County Court who was accused of manufacturing CDS: more than 50 pounds of marijuana. Similar defendants usually see serious jail time. In this situation, based on the facts and Jim's negotiating ability, the judge granted Jim's client an extremely rare "probation before judgement".

Representation in the federal District Court of Maryland of a person accused of importing from China hundreds of thousands of "fake" Viagra and other non-brand sexual pills. The merchandise was imported by pilots at various airports, including Baltimore-Washington International. After many hearings and negotiations with the assistant United States Attorney, and the successful application of several motions, Jim got the case reduced and successfully resolved for the defendant.

Representation of a police officer in Prince Georges County who was accused of various crimes, including a sexual offense. Any sexual conviction would have ruined this officer's career. After various hearings and motions, the case was dismissed, and the officer was able to go back to work.

Representation of a defendant who was being investigated for numerous sexual offenses in Baltimore County. The defendant was not charged but was implicated very heavily, and charges were imminent. Jim got involved in the situation, bringing in additional investigators and applying evidentiary techniques. A young female accused the defendant of performing various sex offenses with her. This defendant—a prominent person in the community and the owner of a large company in Baltimore—claimed innocence. He knew that if the police charged him, his life and career would be ruined. After intervening and dealing with the investigators as well as the state's attorneys, Jim convinced the state's attorney's office not to charge the defendant.

Areas of Practice

Federal Criminal Law
State Courts
Sex Crimes and Registration
Computer Crimes
Assault
Drugs and Distribution
White Collar
Theft
DWI and Traffic
Drug Charges
Weapon and Violent Charges
Domestic Violence
Juvenile Cause
Divorce and Custody
Protective Orders
Child Pornography

Bar Admissions

Maryland Bar, 1992
United States District Court of Maryland, 1994

Education

University School of Law Baltimore Maryland: Juris Doctorate, 1992
University of Baltimore School of Law Baltimore, Maryland: Bachelor of Arts Legal Studies, 1998
Frostburg State College: Bachelor of Science, 1995
Mount St. Joseph High School: High School Diploma, 1980

Honors and Awards

Maryland Super Lawyer Listings, 2014–2017

Top Lawyers Maryland Award Legal Network, 2013
AV Preeminent Martindale Hubble Award, 2005-2017
AV Preeminent Lexis Nexis Peer Review Highest Rating, 2009-2017
Lead Counsel Rating LawInfo.com, 2011-2017
Best of Baltimore Work, Baltimore City Paper, 2011
Past Elected Official State's Central Committee, 1982
Listed Baltimore Leading Firms, Baltimore Magazine

Professional Associations and Membership

Maryland Bar Association, Member
Former County Bar Association, Member
American Association of Justice, Member
Maryland State Central Democratic Committee, Past Member
American Bar Association Section, Criminal Litigation Committee, Member
DUI/DWI Attorney's Member
Criminal Defense Attorney Group, Member
Criminal Defense Lawyer's Group, Member
DUI Defense Lawyers, Member
DUI Law Group, Member
Efface PA Criminal Practice Group, Member
Forensic Science Litigation Attorney Network, Member
American Association for Justice, Inc, Member
National Association of Criminal Defense Lawyers
National Lawyers Guild (NLG)
Solo Attorney Practitioners Forum
The Innocence Project
Trial Lawyer Network for Attorneys and Lawyers
White Collar Criminal Defense Attorneys
American Bar Association

Legal and Political Writing and Speaking Engagements

Identity Fraud; 2012, West Publishing.

Shoplifting Charges in Maryland; January, 2016, Thinking Publication.
The Wimpering of America; January, 2016, Thinking Publication.
Taxes and Jobs; December 2015, Thinking Publication.
Acceptance Speech for the Alumni of the Year Award, Mount St. Joseph High School, 2016. (Speaking on political and social issues.)

Appendix A:
WHAT CRIMES REQUIRE A PERSON TO REGISTER?

Sex Offender Registry Requirements in Maryland

Tier 1: These registrants have been convicted in Maryland of a crime listed below and must register for 15 years. In some situations, it may be reduced to 10.
- Fourth-degree sex offense
- Visual surveillance with prurient intent
- Possession of child pornography
- Engage in illicit conduct in foreign places
- Defile factual statement about a person
- Misleading domain names on the Internet
- Misleading words or digital images on the Internet
- Sex trafficking by force, fraud, or coercion
- Transmitting information about a minor to further criminal sexual conduct
- Travel with intent to engage in illicit conduct

Tier 2: These registrants have been convicted in Maryland of a crime listed below or convicted of a Tier 2 offense in another jurisdiction. They must register for 25 years.
- Abduction of a child under 16 for prostitution
- Distribution of child pornography
- Hiring a minor for prohibitive purpose
- House of prostitution
- Human trafficking
- Sale of a minor
- Sexual conduct between a correctional or DJS employee and an inmate or confined child

- Third degree sex offense
- Sexual solicitation of a minor
- A registrant with two Tier 1 convictions must register in the Tier 2 category

Tier 3: These registrants have been convicted in Maryland of a crime listed below or convicted of a Tier 3 offense in another jurisdiction. They must register for life.
- Assault with intent to rape
- Child kidnapping under the age of 12 or abduction of a child under 12
- Continuing course of conduct for the child
- False imprisonment of a minor
- Forcible sodomy
- Incest
- Kidnapping
- Murder with intent to rape, sexually offend, or sexually abuse a minor
- First-degree rape
- Second-degree rape
- Sexual abuse of a minor
- Sale of a minor
- First-degree sex offense
- Second-degree sex offense
- Third-degree sex offense
- Sexual conduct between a correctional officer or DJS employee and an inmate or a confined child
- Forcible unnatural or perverted practice
- Attempted first-degree rape
- Attempted second-degree rape
- Attempted first-degree sex offense
- Attempted second-degree sex offense
- A registrant with two Tier 2 convictions *or* a Tier 1 and Tier 2 conviction must register in the Tier 3 category.

Appendix B:
OMNIBUS MOTION

STATE OF MARYLAND	*	IN THE
vs.	*	DISTRICT COURT
JIM'S CLIENT	*	FOR
Defendant	*	XXXXXXXXX COUNTY
	*	Case No.: **00-00000000-00**

*   *   *   *   *   *   *   *   *   *   *   *

MOTION PURSUANT TO MARYLAND RULE 4-252

The Defendant, XXXXXXXXXXXXX, by his attorney, James E. Crawford, Jr., Esquire, pursuant to provisions of Rule 4-252, respectfully represents unto this Honorable Court:

1. That all charges against the Defendant be dismissed based upon defects in the institution of the prosecution;
2. That all charges against the Defendant be dismissed based upon defects of the charging document;
3. That all evidence be suppressed because of an unlawful search or seizure;
4. That all wire and oral communications be suppressed because of an unlawful interception;
5. That all judicial and pretrial extra judicial identification be suppressed because they are based upon:
    a   An illegal arrest;
    b.   A violation of the Defendant's right to Counsel;
    c.   A violation of the Defendant's right to due process, because, 1) all identifications were so unnecessarily and impermissibly suggests to give rise to a substantial likelihood of misidentification and, 2) any in Court identification lacks a source

independent of the illegal pretrial confrontation or viewing and constitutes fruits of a poisonous tree;

6. That all admissions, statements, or confessions be suppressed because they were unlawfully obtained;

7. That all trials of all Co-Defendants be severed from the trials of this Defendant.

8. That all offenses pending against the Defendant be severed and tried separately.

9. That any in-court identification of Defendant will be tainted as a result of impermissibly suggestive identification procedures undertaken by police authorities and/or will be the result of an illegal arrest or search;

10. That evidence seized in this case was obtained as a result of an illegal search and seizure and unlawful interception of wire and oral communications;

11. That any statements taken from the Defendant were involuntary or elicited during custodial interrogation without the observance of mandatory procedural safeguards required by law;

12. That the Defendant will be prejudiced by the joinder of this trial with that of any co-defendants and that he will be prejudiced from the joinder of charges arising from separate indictments;

13. That the indictment is defective and/or stale;

14. That this prosecution is barred because of the statute of limitations, immunity and/or former jeopardy.

15. That the Defendant has been prejudiced by lack of a speedy trial.

16. That the State has failed to produce all the documents as required by law in order to ensure the Defendant has a right to a fair trial.

WHEREFORE, the Defendant prays the following relief:

a. That the indictment be dismissed;

b. That any in-court identification be suppressed;

c. That any and all evidence seized by a law enforcement agent be suppressed;

d. That any and all statements allegedly made to a law enforcement agent be suppressed;

e. That the counts of the indictment be severed, and the case be severed from the trial of any co-defendants;

f. Any further relief available under the law.

g. Any identification of the Defendant was illegal and should be suppressed.

h. That the case and all charges be dismissed.

_____
JAMES E. CRAWFORD, JR., ESQUIRE
1435 Sulphur Spring Road
Arbutus, Maryland 21227
(443) 709-9999
Attorney for Defendant

REQUEST FOR HEARING

Defendant requests a hearing on all issues of this Motion.

_____
JAMES E. CRAWFORD, JR., ESQUIRE

STATE OF MARYLAND	*	IN THE
vs.	*	DISTRICT COURT
JIM'S CLIENT	*	FOR
Defendant	*	XXXXXXXX COUNTY
	*	Case No.: **00-00000000-00**

* * * * * * * * * * *

MOTION FOR DISCOVERY & PRODUCTION OF DOCUMENTS

The following requests are made, in accordance with Maryland Rule 4-263, on behalf of the Defendant in the above-captioned action, by his undersigned attorney, and

    a. The requests extend to material and information in the possession or control of the State's Attorney, members of his staff and any others who have participated in the investigation or evaluation of the case and who either regularly report or, with reference to the particular case, have reported to the State's Attorney or his office.

    b. The purpose of these requests is to obtain disclosure of material and information to the fullest extent authorized and directed by Maryland Rule 4-263; and this general purpose shall supersede any language or expression which might otherwise appear to be a limitation upon the object or scope of any request.

    c. Captions or headings used to separate paragraphs are no part of the requests, but are for convenience only.

    d. Material and information discovered by the State's Attorney after his initial compliance with these requests, shall be furnished promptly after such discovery in accordance with Maryland Rule 4-263(h).

    e. These requests are in no way to be considered a waiver of the information required to be furnished without request of the State's Attorney pursuant to Rule 4-263(a) to the Defendant.

    The State's Attorney is requested to:

(1) Furnish to the Defendant: **a)** Any material or information which tends to negate the guilt of the Defendant as to the offense(s) charged; **b)** Any material or information within his possession or control which would tend to reduce the Defendant's punishment for such offense(s); **c)** Any relevant material or information regarding specific searches and seizures (including but not limited to AFR inventory; **d)** Any relevant material or information regarding wire taps and eavesdropping; **e)** Any relevant material or information regarding the acquisition of statements made by the Defendant; **f)** Any relevant material or information regarding pre-trial identification of the Defendant by a witness for the State.

WITNESSES

(2) Disclose the name and address of each person whom the State intends to call as a witness at a hearing or trial to prove its case in chief.

(3) Disclose the name and address of each person whom the State intends to call as a witness at a hearing or trial to rebut alibi testimony.

(4) Furnish the Defendant with the names, addresses and physical descriptions of any person(s) other than the Defendant who were arrested, or otherwise taken into custody, by police or prosecution officials as a possible suspect in this case in which the Defendant is charged.

(5) Furnish the Defendant's counsel with copies of any and all written memoranda which any of the State's witnesses will take with them to the witness stand, or refer to while testifying during the State's case in chief.

(6) Identify, giving home and business addresses and telephone numbers, those persons testifying before the Grand Jury in this case.

STATEMENTS OF THE DEFENDANT

(7) Furnish a copy of each written or recorded statement made by the Defendant to a State agent which the State intends to use at a hearing or trial.

(8) Furnish the substance of each oral statement made by the Defendant to a State agent which the State intends to use at a hearing or trial.

(9) Furnish a copy of all reports of each oral statement made by the Defendant to a State agent which the State intends to use at a hearing or trial.

STATEMENTS OF CO-DEFENDANTS, AND/OR ACCOMPLICES, AND/OR ACCESSORIES AFTER THE FACT

(10) Furnish a copy of each written or recorded statement made by a co-defendant, and/or accomplice, and/or accessory after the fact to a State agent which the State intends to use at a hearing or trial.

(11) Furnish the substance of each oral statement made by a co-defendant, and/or accomplice, and/or accessory after the fact to a State agent which the State intends to use at a hearing or trial. Identify by giving home and business addresses and telephone numbers of the person(s) who heard the statements, or who were within earshot of them. Include dates and places of such statements.

REPORTS OF EXPERTS

(12) Produce and permit the Defendant to inspect and copy all written reports or statements made in connection with the Defendant's case by each expert consulted by the State, including the results of any physical or mental examination, scientific test, experiment or comparison.

(13) Furnish the substance of any oral report and conclusion made in connection with the Defendant's case by each expert

consulted by the State, including the results of any physical or mental examination, scientific test, experiment or comparison.

EVIDENCE FOR TRIAL USE

(14) Produce and permit the Defendant to inspect and copy any books, papers, documents, recordings, or photographs which the State intends to use at a hearing or trial.

(15) Permit the Defendant to inspect any photographs which police or prosecuting authorities may have exhibited to any witness for purposes of identification of the Defendant, and any other photographs which the State intends to use in the trial of the Defendant, and the presentation of its case in chief, and to furnish the Defendant with copies of said photographs, the names and address of witnesses who viewed said photographs, and the results of each viewing of said photographs.

(16) Produce and permit the Defendant to inspect and photograph any tangible objects which the State intends to use at a hearing or trial.

(17) Advise the Defendant as to whether the Defendant was confronted by identification witnesses in any manner other than a line-up while Defendant was in custody of police or prosecution authorities, and if so, to furnish the Defendant with the time, place and circumstances of such confrontation, including the names and addresses of all persons participating in said confrontation.

DEFENDANT'S PROPERTY

(18) Produce and permit the Defendant to inspect, copy and photograph any item obtained from, or belonging to the Defendant, whether or not the State intends to use the item at a hearing or trial.

CONFIDENTIAL INFORMANT

(19) Provide the defense with the names and addresses of any informants, confidential or otherwise, who participated in the

alleged illegal act which is the basis for this Indictment, or who participated in any illegal act which formed any part of the basis for any warrant or process issued and executed in this case, or who participated in any illegal act which was relied upon by any law enforcement official as probable cause to make an arrest and/or search in this case.

AGREEMENT WITH WITNESS

(20) Disclose any promises, understandings or agreements made with any State's witness for his agreement to testify in this case. (*Giglio v. U.S., 92 Sup. Ct. 763, 1972*).

LAW ENFORCEMENT OFFICERS

(21) Provide the defense with the names and assignment of any law enforcement officer, City, County, State or Federal, who participated in any sale, purchase, or negotiation for the sale or purchase of any contraband, said sale, purchase or negotiation having formed any part of the basis for the charge against the Defendant, or any part of the alleged probable cause for an arrest or search involving the Defendant.

(22) Identify (and include duty stations) the members of any police department or other government agency who participated in the investigation, pursuit, arrest or interrogation of the Defendant in this case.

CHAIN OF CUSTODY

(23) Permit the Defendant to inspect any law enforcement report containing the chain of custody of the person of the Defendant, or his property, beginning with the time of Defendant's arrest and continuing throughout the time that the Defendant was in the custody of any police or prosecuting authorities.

(24) Furnish to Defendant, in the event that law enforcement authorities have not prepared the type of report relating to custody of the Defendant or his property, referred to in Paragraph 23, the

names and addresses of all persons who had custody or control of the Defendant, or who participated in the custody or control of the Defendant beginning with the arrest of the Defendant and continuing throughout the time that the Defendant was in custody of any police or prosecuting authorities.

OFFICIAL REPORTS

(25) Furnish copies of any and all statements or reports of prosecution witnesses which have been reduced to writing.

(26) Furnish photostatic copies of all crime laboratory reports pertaining to this case.

(27) Furnish copies of all offense reports or other official police reports pertaining to these offenses.

(28) Supply copies of any and all medical reports that the State has or wishes to introduce into evidence with respect to this case.

(29) Permit Defendant to see, inspect, photocopy and/or copy any photographs, diagrams, blueprints, layouts or plans of the grounds or buildings of the premises involved in these proceedings which are in possession of the State.

(30) Allow the Defendant to see, inspect and view any photographs, film, slides or moving pictures containing relevant evidence in this case which the State has in its possession, or intends to use in the preparation for trial and/or trial in this case.

(31) Produce and permit Defendant to inspect and copy any warrants, affidavits, inventories and other related papers involved in these proceedings.

(32) Furnish to the Defendant a list of all State's witnesses who have criminal records, as well as the alleged victim, giving dates and places of each conviction, the nature of the offense, and the disposition of sentencing.

DEFENDANT'S REQUEST FOR TESTIMONY OF CHEMIST AND ALL OTHERS IN CHAIN OF CUSTODY

(33) The Defendant hereby notifies the State to produce as prosecution witnesses any and all chemists, analysts, and persons

in the chain of custody at the trial in the above-captioned matter, pursuant to Md. Ann. Code, Courts and Judicial Proceedings '10-1000.

>
> JAMES E. CRAWFORD, JR., ESQUIRE
> 1435 Sulphur Spring Road
> Arbutus, Maryland 21227
> (443) 709-9999
> Attorney for Defendant

Appendix C:
MARYLAND TRAFFIC VIOLATION PENALTY QUICK REFERENCE

ZERO-POINT TRAFFIC VIOLATIONS. FINES ONLY

TR 21-1112(d)(2): The cell phone law Maryland recently passed. This law does not have any points as penalties. A driver using hands to use a handheld telephone while a motor vehicle is in motion. (1st offense: $83.00; 2nd offense: $140.00; 3rd offense: $160.00)

TR 21-1004.1 (a): Endangering health, safety, or welfare of a cat or dog by leaving the animal unattended in a vehicle ($70.00). No points for this offense.

TR 21-1001 (c): Stopping vehicle on the highway, with less than 200 feet visibility ($70.00).

TR 21-1003 (i): Stopping, standing, or parking vehicle in highway tunnel ($70.00).

TR 21-205 (c): Obstruction of highway control (device, sign, or signal) ($140.00).

TR 16-105 (b2): Holder of learner's permit driving with an unauthorized person occupying front seat. ($140.00).

TR 16-112 (b): Failure of individual driving on highway to have her license in possession. ($50.00

TR 16-112 (e): Vehicle driver giving a false and fictitious name to uniformed police ($290.00). Big fine but, surprisingly, no points.

TR 14-108 (a): Fraudulent possession of a vehicle (ownership reg. plate, card, title certificate, ID plates) ($290.00). May be a big crime, but no points. Why? The focus is on moving violations, not the severity of the crime itself.

TR 13-401 (h): Driving vehicle on highway with suspended registration ($150.00).

TR 13-401 (j): Driving vehicle on highway with revoked registration ($290.00).

1-POINT TRAFFIC VIOLATIONS

TR 21-103(a): Willfully disobeying a police officer's order/direction/summons. If an accident is involved, the points go from 1 to 3.
TR 21-107(c): Not obeying the direction/order of a school crossing guard.
TR 21-201(a)(1): Failure to obey instructions of properly placed traffic control device.
TR 21-202(c), (e), (k): Failure to yield right-of-way to favored vehicle
TR 21-204(b-d) and (f): Failure to obey a flashing traffic signal
TR 21-303 (b-e): Failure to permit vehicle to pass by speeding up or some other action or improper passing
TR 21-304 (b-c): Passing on the right when not permitted or going off the roadway to pass.
TR 21-305: Driving to the left of center of road where prohibited
TR 21-307(b-d): Driving to the left in a no-passing zone or taking an unsafe left turn in that zone
TR 21-308(a): Failure to drive in a designated direction on posted roadway
TR 21-310(a): Tailgating law: driving too closely
TR 21-312 (a-b): Unauthorized entering or exiting highway
TR 21-401.1: Failure to yield right-of-way at intersection
TR 21-402 (a-b): Failure to yield right-of-way when making a left-hand turn or U-turn
TR 21-405(e): Failure to do what is necessary to make way or make safe passage for an emergency vehicle
TR 21-502-504: Failure to defer to a pedestrian in crosswalk, walking across an adjacent roadway, etc. Depending on the situation, some are zero point violations.
TR 21-1124.1: Text messaging while driving.
TR 21-801(a): The catch-all. Driving at a speed not reasonable or prudent.

TR 21-801-803: Driving from 1–9 miles over the posted speed.
TR 21-804: Driving below the minimum posted speed limit
TR 21-804(c): Driving a limited-speed vehicle on prohibited highway
TR 21-901: Aggressive, negligent, and reckless driving
TR 21-903(c). Driving a motor vehicle on the highway while consuming an alcoholic beverage in a passenger area of a car. Comes with hefty $530 fine.
TR 21-1102: Failure to back up safely

2-POINT TRAFFIC VIOLATIONS

TR 21-202: Failure to stop at a red traffic signal. A few one and zero point violations
TR 21-209: Related failure to stop for red light
21-405(d): Passing an emergency vehicle with its lights on
TR 801.1: Exceeding the posted speed limit from 10–19 miles per hour

3-POINT TRAFFIC VIOLATIONS

Most three-point violations in Maryland are for offenses that would have been one-point violations, but the infraction led to a motor vehicle accident.

TR 21-706: Failing to stop for a school vehicle with activated alternately flashing red lights. A violation also comes with a $570 fine.
TR 16-303 (h-i): Driving on a suspended license, or failure to appear at trial or pay the penalty.

5-POINT TRAFFIC VIOLATIONS

TR 10-105: Failure to report a motor vehicle accident that the law requires to be reported
TR 16-104: Diving a motor vehicle (or moped or motor scooter) on a highway without a license

TR 16-305: Knowingly allowing an unlicensed driver to drive your vehicle

TR 17-107: Driving an uninsured vehicle or letting someone drive your vehicle that you know to be uninsured

TR-21-803: Going more than 30 miles over the speed limit

TR 21–901: Going 85–104mph in a 65mph zone

TR 21-1116: Drag racing

6-POINT TRAFFIC VIOLATIONS

TR 901.1(a) Recklessly driving a vehicle in wanton and willful disregard for the safety of persons and property

8-POINT TRAFFIC VIOLATIONS

TR 21-902 (b)(1) to (b)(2), (c)(1) and (c)(3): Driving while impaired by alcohol or drugs

TR 902.1. Driving within 12 hours after a drunk driving arrest.

- Turning off lights of a vehicle to avoid identification
- Failing to stop after an accident resulting in damage to attended vehicle or property
- Failing to stop after an accident resulting in damage to unattended vehicle or property

12-POINT TRAFFIC VIOLATIONS

TR 14-102: Vehicle theft

TR 16-310 Driver's license fraud

TR 16-303: Driving on a suspended or revoked license

TR 21-902: Driving under the influence of alcohol